IMAGES OF HERTFORDSHIRE

The former gatehouse of Hertford Castle in the grip of a late nineteenth-century winter. Built in 1461–5 it was probably altered shortly after a south wing to the castle was constructed in 1792 and Gothic fenestration added.

IMAGES OF
HERTFORDSHIRE

DAVID MANDER

HERTFORDSHIRE ARCHIVES AND LOCAL STUDIES
SUTTON PUBLISHING LIMITED

First published in the United Kingdom in 1998 by
Sutton Publishing Limited · Phoenix Mill · Thrupp · Stroud · Gloucestershire · GL5 2BU

Hertfordshire Archives and Local Studies, County Hall, Hertford, SG13 8EJ

British Library Cataloguing in Publication Data
A catalogue record for this book is available from the British Library

ISBN 0-7509-1662-1

Half-title page photograph: Jack Piggott at the village pump in the Square, Braughing, *c.* 1930; *title page photograph*: Mrs Williams, her daughter and the gardener in Anstey rectory garden, *c.* 1910. The Rev Frank Ricardo Williams was rector of Anstey from 1907 until the mid-1920s. Anstey rectory once had its own moat, but this had been filled in before 1910.

 ALAN SUTTON™ and SUTTON™ are the
trade marks of Sutton Publishing Limited

Typeset in 11/15pt Baskerville.
Typesetting and origination by
Sutton Publishing Limited.
Printed in Great Britain by
Butler and Tanner, Frome, Somerset.

> *In memory of Harry Dilley,*
> *born a Hertfordshire lad, 1875.*

Goffs Oak from an undated lithograph of about 1840. The elderly tree had another century ahead of it before being blown down in 1950.

CONTENTS

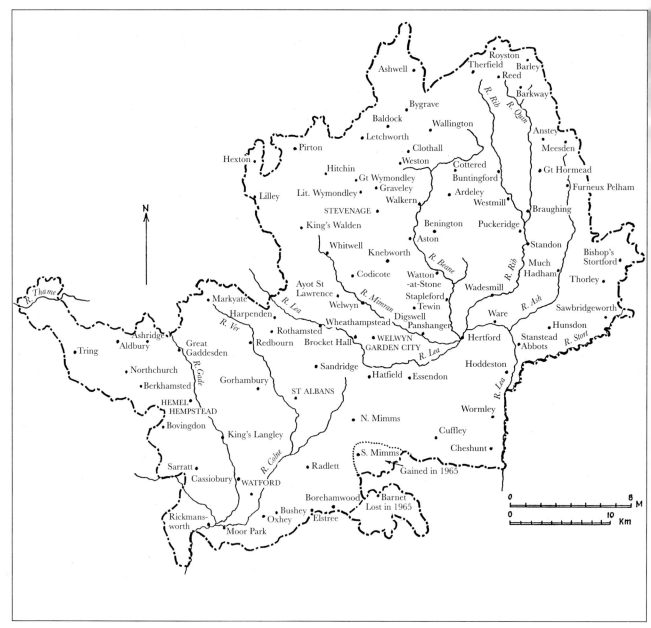

Hertfordshire, *c.* 1977.

INTRODUCTION

'Perhaps Hertfordshire is scarcely intended for motorists . . . Hertfordshire is England at its quietest, with little emphasis of river and hill; it is England meditative.' So thought E.M. Forster as his character Margaret Schlegal speeds along the Great North Road towards Howards End, modelled very closely on Forster's own childhood home, Rooks Nest house, near Stevenage. In 'Two Cheers for Democracy' Forster was clearer in his loyalties about the county:

'Which I still think is the loveliest in England. There is nothing special about it – it is agricultural land, and could not be described in terms of beauty spots. It must have always looked much the same. I have kept in touch with it, going back to it as an abiding city and still visiting the house which was once my home.'

But like most landscapes, Hertfordshire has been thoroughly shaped by its past human inhabitants and although there is a temptation to look back from the upheavals and periods of rapid change that have made up the twentieth century and regard the past, especially as depicted in a book of old photographs, as somehow unchanging,

Bishop's Stortford town, with the spire of St Michael's Church rising above it and the mound of the Waytemore, the former castle of the Bishop of London, in the foreground. (Drawing by W.H. Miller about 1820)

this was not so. Agriculture had gone through a deep depression in the 1870s, which had prevented much investment in buildings, but village and town buildings were not protected by any kind of authority and could be subject to refronting or complete replacement. There were successive waves of country house building after the period of Elizabethan houses before 1580 – in the 1640s and 1650s and a period between 1680 and 1720 that included considerable alteration and modification, as well as the construction of brick town houses like Romeland House in St Albans. The eighteenth-century peak was between 1750 and 1820 and new money was tempted to sweep away or radically reshape older houses. Not even churches were immune, for the mid-Victorian period was the great period of restoration and rebuilding – we are lucky that one photographer recorded work in progress at Therfield.

Hertfordshire was one of the six smallest of the ancient English counties and after the creation of the GLC in 1965 where the principle change was the loss of Chipping Barnet and the acquisition of South Mimms parish, including Potters Bar, it contains 630 square miles. On the north and the north-west the county is bounded by the Chiltern Hills, and on the east by the rivers Lea and Stort. Geologically Hertfordshire lies on a saucer of chalk, with London clay extending to cover part of the county in a line from Watford to Bishop's Stortford. Chalk predominates elsewhere but the north-east corner has glacial deposits of boulder clay and gravel. These glacial deposits also included conglomerate lumps, which are locally known as puddingstones, and a number have ended up on plinths or village greens. The soils in turn have influenced the agriculture – cereal and corn to the north on the chalk and barley on the boulder clay, providing the raw material for the maltings. The county has no large river; the majority of the rivers and streams flow south, with a divide along a line from Rickmansworth to Ware. To the west lie the Colne and its tributaries, the Bulbourne, Gade and Ver, to the east the Lea, Mimram and Stort.

Historically the county has seen different settlement patterns, with a concentration of Roman sites and roads in the west which changed after the Saxon invasions with more small settlements in Domesday concentrated towards the north and the east. The bulk of the land in the north and east was under the plough while land south of St Albans was mainly wooded. There were five towns in 1086 – Ashwell, St Albans and Stanstead Abbots, and Hertford and Berkhamsted (the two latter also having castles). Other towns were creations, like Baldock, which owes its existence to the order of the Templars and takes its name from a medieval transformation of the name of the Near-eastern city, Baghdad. Royston grew round a priory and elsewhere settlements grew at main road junctions, as at Buntingford. At Chipping Barnet the grant of a market to St Albans Abbey in 1199 was important enough for the course of the Roman road to be deflected. River confluences were potential nodal points but towns too close together like Hertford and Ware struggled to see which could attract trade and wealth.

The proximity to London determined the radial roads that crossed the county and prompted the creation of the first turnpike or toll road in England in the seventeenth century in response to the hindrance that roads had become to the movement of goods and people. The dissolution of the monasteries in the 1530s brought royal ownership of estates in Hertfordshire up to 42½ per cent in 1540, but within ten years the vast majority had passed into the hands of new families, men associated with the court for whom an estate close to the capital was a distinct advantage. When money made in the City of London propelled rich merchants to seek a respectable face in ownership of a country estate, Hertfordshire proved equally attractive. Over successive centuries the aristocracy built three palaces – Ashridge, Hatfield House and the lost Theobalds – and many country houses, some successively altered and rebuilt.

Improving the usefulness of the Lea by the construction of the Lea Navigation in the mid-eighteenth century and the construction of what became the Grand Union Canal in 1797–1800 were good for trade, but a greater transformation began with railway construction. The London and Birmingham Railway opened in 1837, the Great Northern Railway through Potters Bar on to Hitchin and the north in 1850; the lines that became part of the Great Eastern Railway reached Broxbourne in 1840, Bishop's Stortford in 1842 and a branch to Hertford was completed in the following year. Last of the main lines was the Midland extension to London via Bedford, opened in its entirety in 1868. Gentry and merchants had been able to preserve close ties with the City, but the relative distance in a pre-railway age prevented daily travel. This gradually changed in the Victorian era, and allowed estate owners to profit, with new developments at Hatfield, Harpenden, Bushey, Watford and many other settlements on the rail network. Canal and railway encouraged local industry – ranging from large and successful industrial concerns like John Dickinson's paper-mills, established in 1804, to smaller concerns like Thomas Blow's beehive factory at Welwyn, an enterprise ended by fire.

In the twentieth century Hertfordshire saw the creation of the first garden city in 1903 on agricultural land in Willian, Norton and Letchworth, after which the new town was named. The principal founder, Ebenezer Howard, went on to buy 1,457 acres of the Panshanger estate in 1919 and this was to become Welwyn Garden City. In the aftermath of the Second World War the new Labour government implemented some of the recommendations of the wartime County of London plan, and designated Stevenage, Hemel Hempstead, Hatfield and Welwyn Garden City as new towns. With the growth in population came changes to transport as branch lines closed and a new network of roads bypassed some towns and cut into the countryside.

Images of Hertfordshire spans some two hundred and fifty years. The use of prints and drawings extends the range of the book back in time to catch something of the appearance of an eighteenth-century country seat, a river crossing, a back street in a country town. The book includes examples of one of the county's pioneering photographers, William Clinton Baker, at work in the early 1850s, but the bulk of the book draws on photographs taken from the 1870s onwards. Some material was commissioned, like the pictures collected by the architect and antiquarian John Laybank Glasscock of Bishop's Stortford to record buildings about to be destroyed for Victorian improvements. The explosion of picture postcards at the turn of the century enabled the recording of towns and villages in times of peace and war. The spread of the portable camera after the First World War increased the recording of domestic scenes and the use of photographs in post-war town guides and in county magazines has preserved images of a county where the car made it easier to explore the lanes and byways but had not yet come to dominate the kerbsides of town streets. A policeman on point duty could form the centre piece of a photograph of Royston, but his presence was a signal that increased traffic was going to change both town and country. School-days and the world of work have not been forgotten – formal class groups, a child on a swing, straw plaiters taking a break outside a cottage door and Thomas Blow's superior beehives all make an appearance. Poverty and charity proved the hardest to illustrate, but the faces of the children outside Hitchin workhouse or in a classroom of the National Refugees Home speak volumes.

The views that have gone to make up this book come from the rich collections built up by Hertfordshire Archives and Local Studies, based at County Hall in Hertford and joined together as a single service from the beginning of 1997. Both collections have been enriched by material donated or loaned for copying by researchers and local residents. In making this selection I have been guided by picture quality, and while I have tried to maintain a balance across the range of themes – towns, villages, the countryside, industry and not forgetting the people who lived in and shaped their local communities – some places are better represented than others, reflecting the strengths of the county collections. Some of the photographs will be familiar from past publications to some readers, but there are pictures that have not been published before. One or two demanded some detective work to tease out a location, date or event, and I hope that some readers will be prompted to contact Hertfordshire Archives and Local Studies with additional evidence of their own. A case in point is the photograph of troops at Watford station on page 136, which I chose for its picture quality, and then had to identify the location and occasion. Quite what troops going to a review at St Albans were doing marching *away* from Watford Junction remains a small mystery.

But I hope that this book will also appeal to those who come to Hertfordshire history for the first time. This has been a voyage of discovery for me into a county that I have passed through and lived in and one which has family ties. My grandfather was born in a cottage in Pixmore, in what is now part of Letchworth, and spent his childhood in the area, while my great-grandmother married a Royston man. At the end of his life my grandfather recalled working as a shepherd boy, having spent much of his working life firing and driving on the Great Northern Railway main line. I hope that there are scenes in this book he would have known and remembered.

In taking a thematic approach to the county, it is inevitable that photographs of individual places are scattered through the book. The index at the back is as thorough as space permits, but it is an index to the pictures. Named individuals are included together with subjects and an indication of locations within a parish or street within a town or village, but references that are in the text only and do not appear in the pictures have not been included. For example, the vicar of Ardeley, the Rev Dr Eck, was the driving force behind the construction of the village hall, and is cited in the caption of the photograph of the hall, but does not appear in the photograph itself and so does not merit an index reference.

I would like to thank Dr Kate Thompson, the County Archivist, Christine Shearman, the Local Studies Librarian and all the staff of the Record Office and Local Studies Library for their help and advice in compiling this work. Thanks are also due to Judith Knight of Watford Library, Melanie Aspey of the Rothschild Archives, Tom Doig, historian of Barkway and to Philip Plumb of Buntingford, former local studies librarian, who provided help and useful advice. I have drawn extensively on the many published works on Hertfordshire local history and am grateful to all authors, living and dead, who have recorded and interpreted the county's past in books and periodicals. Available space precludes a bibliography of sources. I have also drawn on county newspapers, directories and Ordnance Survey maps. The photographs and other illustrations were drawn either from the Local Studies Library collections, the County View series of albums in the Record Office, or from the following collections: D/EBi (Birtchnell Collection); D/ECe (family papers of B.A.L. Cranstone; D/EGl (papers and photographs collected by John Laybank Glasscock).

Special thanks to the following for the reproduction of photographs and views in this book: The Braughing Society Collection and Mr Leslie Piggott (page 1); Edwin Shearing and Dr E.A. Shearing (page 60); Neil Stockton (page 70 bottom); Hertford Museum (page 95 top); The Francis Frith Collection (page 84 top, page 99 bottom, page 100 bottom); Tom Doig (page 156 top).

Copies of views published in *Images of Hertfordshire* can be obtained from Hertfordshire Archives and Local Studies, County Hall, Hertford SG13 8EJ, telephone 01992 555105. If you have historic views of Hertfordshire's past which you think might be of interest and could either be copied or donated, then staff at HALS would be pleased to hear from you.

At the end of *Howards End* Margaret's sister Helen feels that the house, the garden and the big meadow may not remain untouched forever:

'"London is creeping." She pointed over the meadow – over eight or nine meadows, but at the end of them was a red rust. "You see that in Surrey and even in Hampshire now" she continued. "I can see it from the Purbeck Downs. And London is only part of something else, I'm afraid. Life's going to be melted down, all over the world."'

But, within these pages, the red rust was still a distance away and as Helen exclaims, when the big meadow is cut, 'it'll be such a crop of hay as never!' I hope that *Images of Hertfordshire* provides a whiff of forgotten lives, lost scenes where a camera or a sketch pad was at hand to stand in for the times that can be only imagined, as with a boy leading a horse for sale west through narrow country lanes one long summer day in the early 1880s.

David Mander
March 1998

BY ROAD AND RAIL

Hertfordshire owes its pattern of main roads to a range of peoples, from the Bronze Age peoples who established the Icknield Way to the Romans who laid out Ermine and Watling streets. Like the main roads, the railways radiated out from London, supplemented by branch lines built by the competing nineteenth-century companies. But we begin with one of the county's new towns. Letchworth's first bus service provided a link with the main line station at Hitchin. This horse-powered service started from Leys Avenue and is seen here around 1910. A motor bus service to Luton did not begin until 1920.

Hertford from the south-east, with All Saints' Church in the foreground. The poor state of roads led to the creation of turnpike trusts from the early eighteenth century, which maintained main roads and took income from travellers at toll gates. Hertford's roads were run by the Watton trust (from 1757) and the Cheshunt trust (1725) and it is on the latter's turnpike that the postillion is urging the struggling horses in this engraving by E. Dayes published in October 1799. All Saints' Church was destroyed in a fire of 1891.

Hadley Gate.

The Hadley Gate, Barnet, from a postcard sent in August 1911, probably dating from about 1905. Some minor roads remained subject to toll after the bulk of the turnpike gates had been abolished in 1862.

The road mending gang at Sandon, an undated view, *c.* 1920s. Local road repair remained a local matter, passing to newly formed rural and urban district councils after 1894.

Metropolitan Electric Tramways Type 'A' tram car south of St John the Baptist Church, Chipping Barnet High Street, 1912. Tram routes in Hertfordshire were confined to the London fringe area. The Barnet service was established by the MET from Whetstone and the electrified service reached Barnet on 28 March 1907. The tram service was replaced by trolleybuses in 1938.

Edwardian cyclists ready for the off outside the Boreham Wood Motor & Cycle Co.'s shop on the corner of Clarendon Road about 1910. Cycling clubs formed from the 1870s onwards. For women the bicycle helped shake off some of the shackles of Victorian society.

Watford's first bus service began in 1898, running from Bushey Arches to Callowland. As this photograph shows, the vehicle was not exactly purpose built, and had been originally acquired by the Standard Range and Foundry Company to deliver their wares. But moving people must have promised a better return than shifting sundry pieces of metallic produce. Whatever its origins, this was claimed to be Watford's first commercial vehicle.

Essendon Garage, *c.* 1939. Maintaining cars and providing petrol often started from former stabling or smithies. This Essendon proprietor, F.D. Standon, was well sited on the road to Hertford, and was clearly prepared to stay open the long hours needed to attract passing trade.

Something of an obstacle for one motorist was the ford over the Ver at Harpenden Lane, Redbourn, in 1912 – but it made a good excuse for a photograph. In the background is the Midland branch railway from Harpenden to Hemel Hempstead, which ran from 1877 to 1947.

Gipsies tend to be the forgotten people in any county history and then as now were viewed with suspicion. The top view shows what the photographer calls 'Macedonian Gipsies' and their caravan just outside Royston, with a large contingent of the local constabulary in attendance intending to escort them over the county border; the lower is a scene at an encampment on Colney Heath. Both photographs date from around 1904.

The London and Birmingham Railway was the first of the major trunk lines to cross Hertfordshire. This picnic scene was taken on Rowdown above the newly completed Boxmoor station in August 1837. The raised embankment and bridges give some indication of the cost of the route – caused by opposition from local landowners to the original route along the River Gade. (Lithograph by J.R. Jobbins, published August 1837)

Part of the line further south was the impressive viaduct at Watford. There were numerous accidents on the course of the line during construction – the newly opened West Herts Hospital had forty-three cases in the year from July 1836 to July 1837.

The London and Birmingham Railway became part of the London and North Western Railway in 1846. Non-stop expresses needed to replenish their water supply and the solution lay in placing water troughs between the tracks and fixing scoops under the tenders, making a great splash as engine and train passed over. An unidentified Claughton 4–6–0, a class introduced in 1913, and train pass over the Bushey troughs in the mid-1920s.

Railways also ran ancillary services from stations. An LNWR horse-drawn cab is just about to depart from Hemel Hempstead station in the 1880s.

Hitchin station on the Great Northern Railway, July 1881. Mr Pink is standing by his news-stand; behind him on the stairs to the footbridge is Jack Webb, a cab driver and publican at the Coopers Arms. In the centre is Inspector Charles Fisher and porter Teddy Hayward is second from the left.

There was a pause in the construction work for a second railway tunnel on the Midland main line at Elstree in 1895 and navvies pose with track cutting equipment. The new tunnel enabled the main line to be quadrupled at a time of increasing competition between the rival railway companies for traffic and at the culmination of 'The Race to the North' – the attempt to achieve the fastest train to Scotland.

GNR No. 191, a Sturrock 0–6–0 goods engine built between 1851–3, with crew, friends and guests, outside Hitchin shed, photographed by T.B. Latchmore in the 1870s. Enginemen wore white coats in the early days of steam, but would have needed all the protection they could get in their virtually unprotected cabs.

Hitchin engineers have decorated 0–4–2 No. 70 for a special outing. No. 70 was one of two locomotives rebuilt by Patrick Stirling from earlier 2–2–2 engines in 1874. Before the cost of labour rose sharply after the First World War all sheds would have had teams of cleaners to keep engines in pristine condition, but special labours of polishing have been put in to ensure No. 70 did justice to her floral tribute.

GNR 4–4–0 No. 225 on a London-bound train of six-wheel coaches at Hatfield station about 1905. Six-wheelers had been displaced from express trains by this date, so this is probably a stopping train. Hatfield station survived largely unaltered until the major rebuild of 1972.

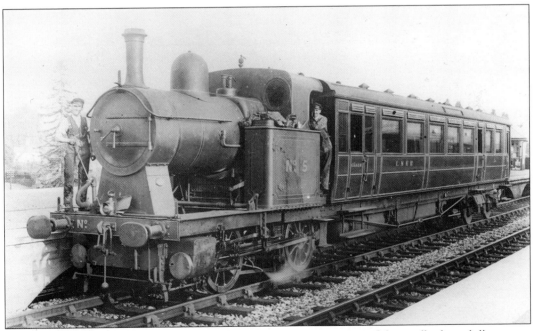

A conventional engine and coaches could be expensive to run on some of the smaller branch lines, even in the days when the railways were the principal form of travel. One answer was the rail motor, a small steam engine permanently attached to a coach. This is GNR rail motor No. 5 at Hertford North station. Four units were introduced in December 1905 after an experiment with small four-wheel petrol vehicles had proved abortive. The coach could hold thirty-two passengers. In the event rail motors proved difficult to service and inflexible, for they often had insufficient power to add coaches at busy times. The Hertford steam railcars lasted about ten years.

Hatfield shed about 1928, with enginemen posed in front of an Ivatt 4–4–0. Standing in front of the engine are Messrs Marsh, Wren, Wilson and Bennett.

The tranquillity of the minor railway station is captured in this view looking west towards Ayot station on the GNR line from Welwyn to Dunstable about 1910. When a fire broke out at the station in July 1948 the fireman had great difficulty in struggling across the fields and the two hour blaze destroyed most of the buildings. The station closed completely in September of the following year.

Stationmaster and staff pose for the camera in a quiet moment at the GNR's Baldock station about 1900.

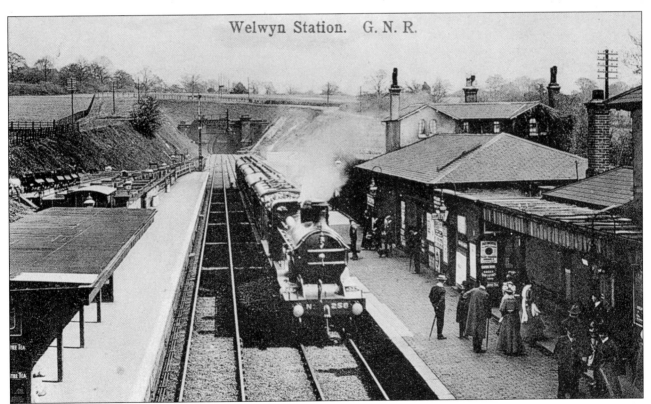

Welwyn station on the GNR in 1907 with an Up stopping train for Peterborough hauled by Atlantic No. 250. Part of the extensive goods yard is visible on the left – almost all freight would have come into Welwyn by rail. On the far left are skips on a contractor's narrow gauge line laid to allow spoil to be removed from a diversion of the Hatfield to Welwyn road made at the expense of George Deering, owner of Lockleys. Both horses and steam locos were used on the line.

Girl Guides provide a line up for Neville Chamberlain, then Minister of Health, clutching his speech (railway stations in our time?) for the opening of Welwyn Garden City's new station in October 1926. Ebenezer Howard had bought 1,457 acres of the Cowper estate at Digswell only seven years before and the first house had been occupied in December 1920.

Ware station on the Great Eastern Railway, built in 1843. The station staff and their families have turned out to be photographed for this view of about 1900, looking towards Hertford. The large goods shed was provided for the maltings traffic. British Rail had intended to demolish the station in the 1970s but in the event it was saved by the joint action of the local council and the Ware Society.

The austere GER station at Bishop's Stortford, taken not long after it had been rebuilt in 1869. The incentive had been the newly completed line from Bishop's Stortford to Braintree, which opened in the same year. Bishop's Stortford's original station had been a train shed built in 1842 when the line was broad gauge. Stationmaster W.J. Anstee (in a top hat) is among the staff group.

The General Strike of 1926 was very divisive, with railway men broadly supporting the industrial action and many of the middle classes stepping forward to act as volunteers to keep services, including the railways, going. The safety regulations of the day did not prevent the railway companies accepting substitute labour. Here the rector of Knebworth and friends are cleaning lamps outside the signal cabin.

Lorries had begun to make an impact on the railways when this view in Welwyn Garden City goods yard was taken around 1936. Containers that have come in by rail are about to be loaded on to a Scammel 'mechanical horse', an electric three-wheel lorry. This was a great advance on the laborious work entailed in shifting separate packages and boxes, though ultimately it was not enough to preserve local goods yards from the onslaught of road hauliers that was to come. The goods shed was demolished in 1986.

Goodbye to all that. A3 Pacific No. 60112 *St Simon* hauls K3 2–6–0 No. 61912 out of Stevenage station on the last weekend of steam out of Kings Cross on 15 June 1963.

WATER EVERYWHERE?

Like the roads, Hertfordshire's rivers were means of communication, and control of traffic on the Lea was the source of fierce contention between Hertford and Ware in the thirteenth century. Travel on the Lea was improved by the construction of the Lea Navigation in the eighteenth century and the Grand Junction Canal was cut through the western half of the county in 1798–9. The smaller streams also provided power for mills, while the position of settlements was determined by the existence of drinkable water, whether from streams or wells. Hertfordshire was also the principal source for London's drinking water after the completion of Sir Hugh Middleton's New River project from Chadwell spring in 1613. This photograph is a reminder that much local drinking water had to be gained the hard way – in this case from the Puckeridge Pump in 1949.

A pause in their labours for the workforce of the Chiltern Hills Spring Water Co., who were constructing new well works at New Ground, Wigginton, near Tring, in the late 1880s. The works were one of the local initiatives of Nathaniel Rothschild, who bought the Tring Park estate in 1872 and founded the water company in the 1880s. Rothschild's initiatives included the construction of new houses on Acreman Street that he handed over to the local council, and these water works provided Wigginton with piped water for the first time.

Chadwell Spring, Great Amwell, is the source of the New River, and was completed by Sir Hugh Middleton to create a new supply of drinking water for London. Repair work was in progress on 12 September 1898.

The New River at Broxbourne. A tranquil summer view looking south towards St Augustine's Church, undated but possibly taken in the 1880s.

The River Lea at Water End to the north-east of Sandridge, where the Roman road from Verulamium, running east towards Ermine Street and the Roman town near the modern Braughing, crossed the river. It remains a minor road and this view from the late 1940s shows the footbridge and ford. (Photograph by Humphrey and Vera Joel)

Another of Hertfordshire's footbridge and ford combinations was at Drayton Ford, Rickmansworth, where the river formed the county boundary between Hertfordshire and Middlesex. This view of 1904 was used as an example of a local beauty spot in the official guide of 1924 although the river had been culverted and the bridge replaced by a road in 1912.

Tiddlers and secrets at Ware, *c.* 1935. The Lea Navigation Act of 1739, which included the construction of locks on the River Lea at Ware, greatly improved traffic in malt and corn sent to London. Brown malt is said to have been the result of an accidental kiln fire in a malting at Ware and the town was the main supplier for London breweries for over 150 years.

Ware and the River Lea looking back towards the position of the view opposite, but taken about thirty-five years earlier. More of the maltings can be seen on the right and beyond them are gazebos, built at the end of the long gardens at the back of the High Street houses either on or projecting over the river. Some have been restored recently.

The River Lea making itself felt at Stanstead Abbots with 1½ foot of it in the High Street, possibly photographed during the bad flooding of June 1903.

The Rye House Hotel stands on the moat of the former Rye House, of which only the fifteenth-century gatehouse remains. The Rye House itself was made famous by a plot of 1683 to assassinate Charles II that cost a number of prominent Whigs their lives, including Lord William Russell. The proprietor of the hotel had lobbied for a station at Rye House to assist his trade. The inn was altered in 1864 when the barge-boarded gables and the large Gothic glazed windows visible in the lower view were added, while the surrounding area was transformed into a pleasure garden in the style of the Vauxhall Gardens. Attractions included the famous Great Bed of Ware. In the upper view the camera has caught a serious attempt to recreate 'Three men in a boat'. The pleasure grounds were sold for development in the 1930s.

Batchworth Lock on the Grand Union Canal as seen in an early nineteenth-century engraving. The canal was completed through Hertfordshire in 1799 and brought change to West Hertfordshire. In nearby mills the Fourdrinier brothers invented a process that allowed the manufacture of paper to be mechanised and the paper to be produced in rolls. Manufacturer John Dickinson leased Batchworth Mills in 1818, taking advantage of the adjacent canal to transport the finished product.

Barges at Batchworth Lock in 1922.

Two barges passing at Iron Bridge Lock, Watford, in 1936. (Photograph by Frank H. Stingemore.)

SCHOOL-DAYS

Until the Education Act of 1870, schooling was the concern of charitable and private schools, strengthened with the foundation of National and British schools by the churches at the beginning of the nineteenth century. This chapter looks at just a few of the county's schools, and some of their pupils, beginning with fun and games at Croxley Green School, Yorke Road, 1902. Built on land given by the paper makers John Dickinson, the school had opened in 1875. It had been divided into boys and girls in 1894, when the boys had moved out to Watford Road. The school finally closed in 1976.

Class II at Faudel Phillips School, Hertford, 1904. The school had been formed two years earlier from a merger of All Saints' Infants' School, founded in 1845, and the adjoining School of Industry for Girls, which had moved to new buildings in 1850. Today only the School of Industry buildings survive.

Applecroft School, Welwyn Garden City: Miss Southwell and Class VIII, 1930. Applecroft was the first school to open in Welwyn Garden City in 1923, though it was not completed until 1926. It marked a radical departure from schools of the time, with its light and brightly painted classrooms, whose folding glass doors allowed conversion to open-air classrooms in the summer, while pupils could grow their own flowers and vegetables in a quarter of an acre of school garden.

Exercise time for the girls at Hitchin British School, *c.* 1900. The school had been founded by William Wilshere in 1810 in Dead Street (later Queen Street) and the girls' school followed nine years later. New buildings were put up in 1857 and by 1913–14 average attendance at the girls' school was 156. The school is now owned by the Hitchin British School Museum Trust.

Ashwell Board School about 1900, looking from the corner of Bear Lane. Ashwell's first school had been founded by a bequest made to the Merchant Taylors' Company in 1681, but the Company was not prepared to allow it to be used to enable Ashwell to meet the obligations of the Elementary Education Act of 1870. Most landowners were opposed to selling land for the new school, which was built in 1878 to the design of Henry George Luff, and the opening was marred by a row between the Rector and Mr Flitton, an opponent. A rise in the birth rate in the late 1860s and 1870s had made the school necessary, though provision was basic – plain distempered walls above dark stained matchboarding, and outside toilets that froze in winter.

The rear of Ware Grammar School for Girls, *c*. 1906. In that year, the school had taken over the former Amwell House of *c*. 1730, once owned by John Scott, the Quaker poet. In 1908 one local girl, who attended a different school, was reported as being very envious of the amenities the school offered – tennis, hockey and a gymnasium! The buildings survive among twentieth-century college additions, but the school moved out in 1965.

Watford National School in Church Street was built in 1841 and this engraving by George Hawkins was produced around the time of opening. The school closed in 1922 and after a period as company offices, when it was re-named Almond Wick (after adjoining land near the almshouses), it became the local register office. It was demolished in the 1960s and the site is now a car park.

The adventurous Miss Baker, teacher at Preston School, and her motorbike, *c.* 1930s.

A class at Preston School, *c.* 1930s. Preston School had been built by Thomas Harwood Darton in 1849, originally intended to serve as both a day and a Sunday school. In 1947 it became a voluntary primary school, having merged with the neighbouring Langley School in 1939.

Pupils at St John's School, Lemsford, in costume for a school play, *c.* 1900. The school had been built in 1872 with funds from the owner of the Panshanger and Brocket estates, who continued to support it until 1903. Like many village schools St John's closed for seasonal absences, which included not only the harvest but also the annual autumn nutting expedition to Brocket Park. There was nowhere for the children to eat their lunch until a benefactor donated money for a canteen in 1906, and there were no school meals until 1942. In 1919 the *Daily Mail* financed a bee club and the children visited the neighbouring factory at Welwyn.

Group from the village school at Great Hormead in 1932. Back row, left to right: Owen Canfield, Ted Biggs, Alf Canfield, Melvin Taylor, Jack Huckle and George Shadbolt. Middle row: Percy King, Bert Wilson, Frank Adams, Lucy Bentley, Frieda Burleigh, Doris Driver, Sylvia Driver, Meg Shadbolt, Molly Johnson, George Mastall and Victor Hunt. Front row: ? Wilson, Muriel Barnes, Lily Clark, Irene Shadbolt, Hilda Williams, Dorothy Hummerstone and Edith Brett.

GRACIOUS LIVING

Being close to London made Hertfordshire an ideal county for a landed estate for those whose business lay at court in the sixteenth and early seventeenth centuries, and today the county has a fine range of country houses that survive from the period. The coming of the railway made it easier for nineteenth-century City merchants and businessmen to make their homes in the county, and they bought existing estates or, like the Rothschilds, built new ones. One of the grandest of the county's houses was Hatfield House, above, built for Robert Cecil in 1607–12. This view by J.D. Harding was taken from the south-east of the house while an archery meeting was in progress. It may date from shortly before the fire of 1835 that gutted the west wing of the house.

Theobalds Park was built for George Prescott in 1763 and is seen here in a late eighteenth-century painting by Francis James Sergent. The house was considerably altered in the nineteenth and twentieth centuries by the Meux family, who had Temple Bar transported from London to act as an entrance to the park (see page 54). The contents were sold after the death of Lady Henry Bruce Meux in 1911.

Gobions House, North Mimms, seen from the south-west looking across the lake. Gobions House lay to the south of the present Brookmans Park. It had originally belonged to the More family but after a succession of merchant owners it was sold to Jeremy Sambrook in 1707, who employed architect James Gibbs to remodel the house and Charles Bridgeman to redesign the gardens. Gobions was sold to the owner of the neighbouring Brookmans in 1838, who had added the grounds to his estate. The house was demolished and only the Folly Arch remains.

Cheshunt Great House in Goffs Lane was built for Antony Denny in the fifteenth century. By the early 1960s, when the top view was taken, it had been reduced to one wing of a courtyard house with the fifteenth-century hallway beyond. This part of the house had been encased in brick between 1762–72 and was altered again in 1806. The lower view, a lithograph by W.H. Taylor, shows the hall with its wind braces as it would have appeared in the mid-1850s, and a visiting Victorian family. Sadly, the house was destroyed by fire on 6 September 1965 and only the cellars remain today, incorporated into a sunken garden.

Moor Park, near Rickmansworth, from the air, *c.* 1950. Moor Park was originally built for the Earl of Bedford in the seventeenth century but between 1725–7 was extensively remodelled for Benjamin Styles, probably by Sir James Thornhill, who made it one of the county's grandest eighteenth-century houses. The formal gardens date from 1830–40. A golf club had used the grounds from 1910 and remained after the house was sold in 1919.

Danesbury, Welwyn, with the Blake family on the lawn about 1851. The house was originally St John's Lodge, built about 1778, but after banker William Blake bought it in 1824 he had it extensively altered and renamed. The Blakes sold it in 1919 and it later became a hospital. The photograph was taken by William Clinton Baker of Bayfordbury.

The entrance hall to Moor Park, photographed by Frederick Downer in the 1890s. The entrance hall ran up to the whole height of the house, and was hung with paintings by Jacopo Amigoni, a Venetian living in England from 1729–36, which follow the story of Io. The ornate door-case is probably also the work of Italian artists. Moor Park was the seat of Lord Ebury, but the Grosvenor family sold it in 1919 to Lord Leverhulme, who intended to create a country club out of the house and estate. Subsequently in the late 1950s part of the estate was sold for housing.

Bayfordbury, just to the north of Bayford, originally dates from 1759–62, built for William Baker, but was extensively reworked in 1809–12 by the second William Baker. The top view shows one of the cedars planted in 1765 at the rear of the house and the orangery about 1851. The people are Mrs Ann Baker and her guests Sir Bootle and Lady Boothby. The gardens were justly renowned. The lower view catches the Baker children on the garden portico, with part of the iron balcony that runs along this frontage just visible. Both photographs were taken about 1851 by pioneer photographer William Clinton Baker. The house was sold to the John Innes Institute in 1939 and, after a period in college hands, is now the headquarters of the building firm, Rialto Homes.

Cassiobury House, Watford, seen in the top view about 1900, was built for Sir Richard Morrison shortly after 1547 and was remodelled in 1674–5 and again in 1800 when James Wyatt gave it a touch of Gothic. The lower view shows the drawing-room about 1860. One young girl in service in the house just before the First World War was part of a staff of twenty, and there were some thirty gardeners. The Earl of Essex sold the house and its contents in 1927 and it was later demolished. The entrance lodge survived until 1970, but although the extensive grounds survive as a public park only the former Dower House survives.

The stables at Hatfield House, drawn by Holland Tringham in 1900. This was all that remained of Bishop Morton's palace of *c.* 1480–90, most of which had been demolished when Hatfield House was built. The splendid timber roof is one of the best medieval survivals in the county. The former palace remained in use as a stable from 1628 to the early twentieth century; it is now part of the banqueting facilities at Hatfield House.

The Japanese garden at Cottered was created by Herbert Goode (1865–1937) in 8 acres attached to his house Cheynes, and was inspired by a visit he made to Japan in 1906. In 1923 landscape artist Seymon Kusumoto came from Japan and designed additional buildings and bridges over the next three years. The estate was sold after the death of Goode's widow in 1964 and The Garden House built on it in 1966. In recent years there have been efforts to restore the gardens to their glory of seventy years ago.

THE LAND

Pedigree pig sale in the barn of Buttermilk Hall Farm, Buntingford, May 1950. Many of the great county estates drew substantial revenue from their tenant farmers and the 1870s proved a difficult time as competition from American wheat undermined British farmers. Farms were hard to let, new building virtually ceased and there was a 50 per cent increase in pasture. Profit margins remained narrow, though there were signs of recovery in the Edwardian years. This chapter provides a small sample of farming and associated activities.

Pigeons formed an important supplement to the diet and special provisions were made on some estates. This is the dovecote at Manor Farm, Walkern, an octagonal brick building dating from the late seventeenth century, photographed about 1910 and still preserved today.

Threshing at Church Farm, Aldbury, about 1905. The introduction of steam power greatly helped with the harvest but did not greatly diminish the need for extra seasonal labour.

A break during haymaking, possibly also taken at Church Farm in the same year. The women would have been kept busy getting cans of tea for the men. In the 1920s general labourers on the farm would have received 15 shillings per week. Post-war workers included George and Phillip Fleckney and Messrs Baldrich and Collier.

Italian prisoners of war working for the Darling family on the harvest on Greys Farm, near Therfield Heath, about 1947. There were five Italian POWs assigned to the farm. There was a POW camp at Royston Heath from 1940 and prisoners were sent out to the neighbouring farms. This was the last English harvest they laboured on, for the camp closed in June 1948.

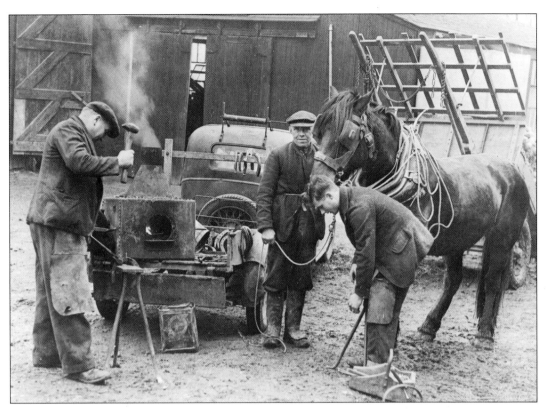

A smith hammering a new shoe on a mobile forge at Pentlow Farm, Braughing, while the horse stands by, *c.* 1950.

Sutes farmhouse lies just north of High Cross, Standon. In this view taken about 1914, the farmer has brought his three-horse team up a track in front of the surviving section of the moat that partly encircles the house. There was a house here in 1412, though the present timber-framed and part weatherboarded house probably dates from the sixteenth century. Sutes was once a manor house. Sutes manor was bought by Robert Bird in 1677 and passed to four co-heirs in 1732. David Powell, husband of one of them, bought out the others in 1745 and thereafter Sutes formed part of a wider estate. Today it is a family run farm. Sadly, the elms have gone, victims of Dutch Elm disease.

Local woodlands provided more than just firewood. Here two farm workers are cutting and bundling pea-sticks in Park Wood near Bramfieldbury in the 1930s. Park Wood was created as a hunting park and was home to Richard de Park in 1294. Some hunting parks resulted in the disappearance of villages and by 1485 there were forty such parks in the county.

The Enfield Chase hunt sets off from Temple Bar, at the edge of Theobalds Park, in the 1950s. Temple Bar was designed by Sir Christopher Wren in 1672 to replace the earlier City of London gate destroyed in the Great Fire. It was the last of the old city gates to survive. It was dismantled in 1878 and acquired by Sir Henry Meux for his Hertfordshire estate. In recent years the statues were removed for restoration and the building was boarded up.

INDUSTRY

W.H. Cranstone's stand at a Cambridge trade fair in the 1890s. Cranstone & Co. began as an ironmongery business at 25 High Street, Hemel Hempstead, in 1798. After merging with another family firm it came into the control of William Henry Cranstone, whose employees here are about to demonstrate one of their frictionless hoists. Much of Hertfordshire's pre-twentieth-century industrial activity was on a small scale, but there were some exceptions, notably the paper-making activity of John Dickinson and his successors at Apsley and nearby mills. New towns like Welwyn Garden City needed to attract businesses to provide local employment and Hertfordshire had its own special place in the history of British film making.

Straw plaiters outside their cottage at Titmore Green, south of Little Wymondley. Straw hat making went back to the sixteenth century in the county and straw plaiting provided employment for 8,598 women and 608 men in 1861. It paid better than agricultural work but it did not lift workers from poverty.

Agricultural produce provided one enterprising woman with employment. Mrs Kingham of Heronsgate packed hampers with rabbits and poultry. Heronsgate, near Chorleywood, had begun as O'Connorville, created by the Chartist Fergus O'Connor as a co-operative estate in 1847. When it failed in 1851 the cottages were sold off to private buyers.

Samuel Wilson, wheelwright, and his son William repair a cartwheel at Breachwood Green, south-west of Kings Walden, in the 1890s. Mr Wilson snr established his business before 1878 but it had disappeared by 1910.

Ogglesby and Son's smiths works at Harpenden before the First World War. The business was founded in 1873 by Charles Ogglesby and made a variety of products including cycles. Family members later became motor dealers in Harpenden.

Ebenezer Boorman, his family and employees are gathered outside the Cromer smithy and forge, Ardeley, about 1898. The impressive array of equipment in front of the house would appear to include a static boiler.

The outside of the Welwyn Beehive Works, with every home comfort for the industrious bee spread out on display. Thomas Blow established his 'Steam Works' next to the Great Northern Railway in the mid-1880s after extensive foreign travels to broaden his bee-keeping experience. He designed some of his own machinery and his workforce made wooden and traditional straw skeps. A fire virtually destroyed the works in August 1898 – the combination of timber, beeswax and fuel oil proved so flammable that the telegraph poles on the adjoining main line caught fire and an express train was delayed for twenty minutes. The Welwyn brigade under Captain Blow did its best but the Hatfield brigade had an accident on route and was delayed. The fire marked the end of the business, though a successor, run by Edward Taylor, was based at Digswell by 1902.

Sand used in the construction of Welwyn Garden City was extracted locally. Much of it came from Twentieth Mile Pit near Stanborough Lane, one of a number of quarries linked by a 2 foot narrow gauge railway that opened in 1920. The line used Motor Rail internal combustion engines and this view shows one at the Twentieth Mile Pit around 1938. By that stage most of the system had closed and only the line from Digswell to Twentieth Mile Pit remained; it too closed around 1940.

Steam delivery lorry in the Brewery Hill yard of Pryor Reid & Co., *c.* 1910. The Hatfield brewery dated back to the seventeenth century but was bought by John Morris and Alfred Pryor, Quaker brewers from Baldock, in 1836. Alfred was sole proprietor at his death in 1876 and the business passed to his son Edward and son-in-law Charles Reid and became Pryor Reid & Co. King Edward VII once availed himself of a barrel seat in the yard when his car broke down outside the brewery! Sadly, Reid's son was killed during the First World War and Charles Reid sold the business and its tied houses in 1920. The site was sold to a garage and is now the site of Salisbury Square.

Charles Harrowell owned a small brickworks at Shootersway, outside Berkhamsted. The top view shows a group of 'crowders' by the Scotch kiln in 1935; the lower the drying sheds in 1934, with Harry Watts, the yard manager, on the left, Charles Harrowell on the right and Charles' daughter Betty between them.

Interior of the Testimonial Laboratory at Rothamsted Experimental Station about 1912. Founded by John Bennet Lawes in 1843, the station had been so successful in producing artificial fertilisers that a group of grateful Hertfordshire farmers got up a subscription for a testimonial in 1853, which raised £1,200 and which went towards the construction of the laboratory in the following year.

By contrast a more traditional scene at the rear of Ickleford Mill on the River Oughton, probably in the late 1880s. The mill had been owned by the Priest family from before 1851. It was rebuilt by Thomas Priest in 1892, who installed steam and roller mills. The large mill-wheel was scrapped during the Second World War, and the mill was electrified and further rebuilt in 1955, with silos added for bulk storage. Yet another mill was built in 1969.

John Dickinson, a London stationer, set up his first paper-mill at Apsley Mill in 1804. Two years later he bought Nash Mill. Further expansion was financed by the invention of a non-smouldering cartridge paper, which was used in the Penisular War and at Waterloo, and a modified version during the Crimean War of 1853–6. A Dickinson silk thread paper was used for postal stationery after the introduction of the uniform penny post in 1840. A third mill was added in 1825 at Home Park. After 1818 all Dickinson's factories were served by canals. This view, from the turn of the century, shows paper production at one of the mills.

A group of Indian princes came over for Queen Victoria's Golden Jubilee in 1897. John Dickinson offered them hospitality at his house, Abbots Hill, near Abbots Langley. This view shows the party on Kings Langley and Abbots Langley station.

Rag sorting at one of Dickinson's mills about 1910. By 1911 Nash Mills was the largest producer of white and tinted boards in Britain. The mills produced munitions during both world wars and after the Second World War the site at Apsley Mill was extended to cover over 30 acres.

Among the more agricultural trades was Ryders the seedsmen at St Albans, established at Holywell Hill shortly before 1906. Ryders was the first company to produce small packets of seeds. This view shows staff counting and packaging seeds in the company's purpose-built works at Holywell Hill. Ryders has long gone but the building survived in use by the Post Office until the late 1980s.

Welgar was one of the earliest companies to set up in Welwyn Garden City, opening its shredded wheat factory in 1926. Established in England in 1908, the firm chose a site alongside the railway and took on 100 employees. The top view shows Joseph Bryce, the managing director, and his staff on the front steps of the factory shortly after the opening in that year. The new factory was described as 'a palace of crystal, its great walls held together by slender white tiled columns of concrete'. The lower view shows part of the assembly line in the 1920s. So closely associated was shredded wheat with Welwyn Garden City that people even named the product instead of the town when buying a railway ticket. The company was bought by Nabisco in 1938.

It was imperative for the new garden city at Welwyn to attract industry. It was recognised that small concerns and firms developing a product might be attracted and units were put up that could be easily sub-divided as individual tenants required. Among the businessmen who came was Frank Murphy, who was developing radios in 1928. Some businesses were even humbler. These women were making toys in the late 1920s in one of the wooden huts used for a multiplicity of functions in the early days of Welwyn Garden City.

In 1922 Captain H.R.S. Birkin established a factory, opposite the Cherry Tree Restaurant, to research and experiment on car engines in Welwyn Garden City. Birkin was also a racing enthusiast and won the 24 hour Le Mans race in 1929.

Charles Everett's coach-building works at Holywell Hill, St Albans, possibly in the late 1890s. Everett had begun as a coach painter in 1862. By 1878 he was also building carriages and by 1890 had a showroom on Holywell Hill and an additional works in White Hart Yard. Everett died around 1906, but the business carried on until shortly after 1929.

Although the film sets at Elstree and Borehamwood were more famous, over eighty films were made at Welwyn Garden City between 1932 and 1942. The studio was established by the British Instructional Film Company in 1928 and closed in 1952. It was later to become part of the factory that made Polycell. Cast and crew of *Double Error* pose on the set.

VILLAGES

Like most counties Hertfordshire has a variety of village types – nucleated settlements centred round a green or church, street villages strung out along a main road or, notably in the north-east of the county, areas of isolated farmsteads linked by winding lanes and paths. We begin with a glimpse of post-war village life – two women cyclists with bikes and hoes in the village street of Furneaux Pelham in 1950. There was little to disturb the peace other than traffic from Rayment's brewery and the odd delivery vehicle. (Photograph by G.L. Blake)

The ford and bridges over the River Rib at Wadesmill – a late eighteenth-century view drawn by R. Batty. Wadesmill was one of the three places in Hertfordshire chosen to impose tolls in 1663 and was the only successful one, pioneering the wider introduction of turnpikes sixty years later.

Bell Bar village street, North Mimms, drawn by J.C. Buckler about 1840. The tall farmhouse at the end is the present Elm Tree Farm, but the cottages in the foreground were demolished to build new housing in the post-war period. The lane was formerly part of the Great North Road and it is possible that Elm Tree Farmhouse may once have been a pub called the White Hart.

St Katherine's Church, Ickleford, from the Turnpike Lane corner in the late 1880s. The church dates from *c.* 1150 and has a thirteenth-century tower. The sign of the Old George, a sixteenth-century building facing the green, is just visible. In front is John Buckingham's smithy. Buckingham's father had been the village smith in 1838 and he had been an apprentice to another smith in 1851. He became the first surveyor of the roads and assistant clerk to the newly created parish council in 1894. Arthur Hopkins eventually took over Buckingham's smithy, and kept it on until just before the Second World War.

Great Amwell village, from the north, about 1900. To the right behind the trees is the small church of St John the Baptist with its Norman apse and monuments to the Mylne family – Robert Mylne was one of the engineers of the New River Company. The house on the left is the Grove, which Mylne built for himself in 1795–7. It was largely destroyed in a fire in the early part of this century and rebuilt to a different design. Just below the church is the course of the New River and a view out over the Lea valley.

An early nineteenth-century drawing from the lane that runs west out of Essendon. The house in the foreground was the Salisbury Crest public house. Just beyond is the fifteenth-century tower of St Mary's Church. The Salisbury Crest may have begun life as the King's Head, in existence in 1654; certainly parts of the present building date from the seventeenth century. It changed its name between 1817 and 1820. The pub closed in 1994 and was still in the throes of building works four years later, intended for private housing.

The cottage garden of Southfields on the south side of Ackerman Street, Little Hadham, about 1900.

Mrs Gravestock stands by the stocks on the green at Aldbury about 1905. The stocks survive today and lend a note of period charm to the village, but in the seventeenth century they would have been well maintained and served as a visual deterrent to local malefactors.

A water cart in Stocks Road, Aldbury, in the 1890s. Most of the village's drinking water came from Lord Brownlow's well in Chantry Row, though villagers also drew on neighbours who had their own wells or even took their water from the pond. The summer of 1897 was an especially dry one, and more of the villagers must have been dependent on Lord Brownlow's water cart.

A glance at his handiwork from a Gilston villager on a summer's day at the turn of the century, as he emerges from the garden on the north side of Pye Cottages at Pye Corner. Local farm labour was supplemented by gipsies up to the end of the 1930s, coming for the corn harvest, pea picking and lifting sugar beet. Rebuilding from the mid-Victorian period has replaced many of the houses that pre-dated 1850. One of the casualties was the home of the gardener, a thatched cottage a little to the south, on the other side of Fiddlers Bridge.

The Plume of Feathers, Pye Corner, Gilston, *c.* 1900. This pub was recorded in 1661 when the landlady was charged with suffering 'evil rule', selling tobacco and not attending church. In the eighteenth century it was owned by the Plumer family and when a Plumer widow married one Robert Ward in 1827, he assumed the name Plumer Ward. The pub was the Plumer Ward Arms in 1852 but the Plume of Feathers by 1892. A spate of road accidents led to heavy crash barriers being installed on the roadside in the 1980s.

This could have been a chapter end to one of Thomas Hardy's novels but is merely a record of the demolition of cottages at Church End, Little Hadham, in 1903 as recorded by W. Minet. The cottages stood on the north side of the path to the church and the site was being cleared to build a new house.

The Wilson family and friends in the yard of their house, No. 2 High Street, Barkway, around 1900. On the left side of the cart are, from left to right, Frank Thrussell, Howard Wilson, Fred Simmons, Mr Parrot jnr, Timmy Nottage and Mr Parrot snr. In front of the cart is Frank Maclon; alongside him in the tall hat is Mr Wilson. His wife and their three children, Oswald, Margaret Alice and Winifred, stand by the gate and leaning on the fence are Wilfred and Priscilla Wilson.

The mill at Mill Green, Hatfield, in the late 1940s. Built around 1762 and once used as a fulling mill, by the 1940s the mill race passed through a disused building for milling had ceased in 1911. Today the former miller's house is a local history museum and the mill has been restored to working order.

Much Hadham village street about 1900. Beyond the house with the hipped roof is Morris Cottage. This had once been a hall house dating from the mid-fifteenth century and was home to William Morris' sister in the later nineteenth century. The architect Phillip Webb restored it and extended it at the rear.

Graveley village street about 1905. Photographer Francis Frith has persuaded a good collection of local children to enliven the scene. Graveley was on the Great North Road due north of Stevenage and it took the construction of the A1(M) to restore some peace to the village after traffic growth in the 1950s and 1960s.

A glimpse of the early fifteenth-century church of St Mary, Braughing, about 1949, taken from Ford Street. On the right is the back of the Old Boys' School, a sixteenth-century building with brick nogging between the exposed beams. This photograph featured for a number of years on the front cover of Braughing's local guides, promoting its reputation as one of Hertfordshire's most attractive villages. (Photograph by G.L. Blake)

The village hall at Ardeley from across the pond, 1950. Ardeley Green was the creation of J. Howard Carter in 1917, together with the surrounding terraces that were designed by F.C. Eden at the same time. The vicar, Dr H.V.S. Eck, the incumbent from 1916–21, was the force behind the creation of the hall, also designed by Eden. Eck got Carter to donate the land and organised local volunteers, including farmers, to transport materials from the station. The hall opened in November 1919. (Photograph by G.L. Blake)

Another village green, this view of Westmill dates from around 1950. The church of St Mary has a surviving Saxon wall but was extensively restored in the nineteenth century. The house with the bay is Parliament House, dating from the seventeenth century. The remainder of the row is said to have been built by Samuel Pilgrim in the early eighteenth century. The pump under the shelter has featured in many photographs of the village. (Photograph by G.L. Blake)

Children in Bramfield village street, 1927. The view was taken looking south across one corner of the crossroads in the village centre. The building in the distance is the present post office.

Bengeo is now part of Hertford but it was once a distinct settlement east of the River Beane. This is Port Hill from just south of the Reindeer Tavern at the turn of the century. The Reindeer dates back to 1740, though it began life as the Running Deer and was so named until about 1837. The wall on the left is part of a disused Quaker burial ground.

Cottages on the east side of Puckeridge High Street, in the part that then formed part of Braughing parish. This view dates from around 1910. At one time one of the cottages was home to Bert Mottram. Alternatives to thatched cottages, which had few amenities, were beginning to be considered in the years before the First World War. Much Hadham gained its first council houses in 1914.

The school at Standon and the Puddingstone about 1910. The school, which closed in the 1960s, has been identified as the school established by the Knights of St John, who held the parish from the late twelfth century and also had a commandery and a hospice here. The stone (puddingstone is a local name for glacially deposited conglomerate) was resited from a place in the church wall in 1904; another one in the village marks the place where Vincent Lunardi landed after the first balloon flight in England in 1784.

Elstree was originally a ribbon development along Watling Street and did not become an independent parish until 1909. The top view was taken in Barnet Lane about 1910–11 and shows the new dining-rooms and E.L. Staples' shop. The lower photograph, dated 1939, shows part of the main church and the church of St Nicholas, largely the work of P.C. Hardwick in 1853 but incorporating parts of the fifteenth-century church. The school in the foreground dates from 1882–3. Still's Cottage and Roger's Cottage, between the church and the school, were demolished in 1953.

TOWNS

Hertford, the county town, maintained its position despite competition from Ware, as it remained the site of a royal castle and a chartered borough. St Albans was the creation of the abbey, away from the former Roman town of Verulamium, which was gradually destroyed. Other towns owe their origins to organic growth at key road junctions, like Buntingford, or to a planned act, like the foundation of Baldock by the order of Knight Templars. In the twentieth century Hertfordshire saw the creation of two new garden cities and the expansion of older towns, like Hemel Hempstead. A procession outside the Corn Exchange, Hertford, possibly part of the local celebrations for Queen Victoria's Diamond Jubilee in 1897.

White Horse Street, Baldock, in the early 1920s. Fred Butler has used tyres as an advert outside his garage. Butler began selling cycles in the late 1890s. They became increasingly popular in the next ten years, and people bought them (paying by instalment) and practised in the High Street at lunch times. There were some accidents – one man couldn't negotiate the corner with White Horse Street and crashed into the harnesses outside a saddler's! That bike went back to Butler's.

White Horse Street and the early fourteenth-century tower of St Mary's Church, Baldock. The pub in the centre is the Sun, after which Sun Street, leading to the church, took its name. It was so named by 1806, but became the Victoria at some date between 1862 and 1889 and was rebuilt around 1930. The tall three-bay brick building became No. 13 White Horse Street and gained its brick front (behind the stucco) in the eighteenth century; with an altered door-case, it survives today. (A Buckler drawing from about 1830)

A view of the King's Head, Bishop's Stortford, drawn and engraved by C.L. Tyler and published in May 1828. Tyler was standing at the end of North Street looking down Market Street. The King's Head had been one of the town's principal inns, where the justices of the peace held petty sessions, but competition from the Crown and increased rowdiness of the clientele both affected trade. The sessions were moved to the King's Head at Hockerill and the King's Head, Bishop's Stortford, was demolished in 1825 to make way for the new Corn Exchange of 1828.

Berkhamsted High Street, with trade union parade in the early 1920s.

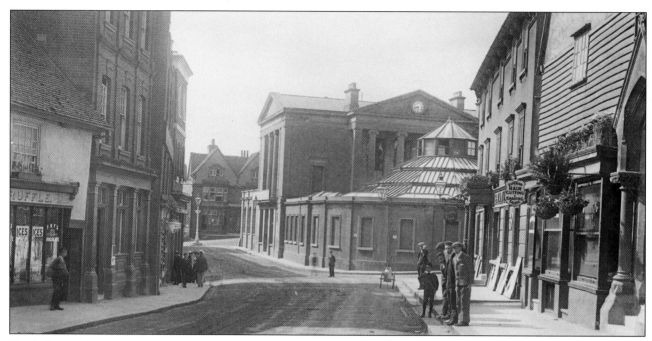

North Street, Bishop's Stortford, *c.* 1902, looking towards the Corn Exchange, designed by Lewis Vulliamy. Originally this frontage had had a grand entrance presided over by a statute of Ceres, goddess of the harvest, but these were removed and a glass roof substituted over the curved end to provide light for the grain dealers' rooms. The porch on the right is the entrance to the Urban District Council offices. (A Francis Frith view)

The London and County Bank also occupied part of the Corn Exchange, Bishop's Stortford. Bank clerks pose in their top hats in Market Square, *c.* 1865. (Photograph by L. Bing)

North Street, Bishop's Stortford, from the Corn Exchange in the late 1860s. The properties beyond the gabled building next to the Half Moon Inn housed the businesses of Samuel Morley, tailor, and John Spooner, draper; both had moved by 1869 and the site ultimately became the Urban District Council offices. The Half Moon Inn had been on this site since 1752; in 1865 the landlord, Henry Parish, had claimed that the concern of the Highways Board about the smell emanating from his premises was greatly exaggerated! The street lighting seen in this view dates from the early 1840s.

The Cock Inn at the top of Hockerill Street, Bishop's Stortford, with a selection of locals in the mid-1870s. Edwin and Eliza Eyre's drinking fountain was erected in 1872. The Cock may date from the mid-sixteenth century and was traditionally used by servants, while their masters put up at the Crown or the Red Lion. Each of the four corners of the crossroads at Hockerill had an inn in the eighteenth and early nineteenth century but not all survive.

Two views of the houses at the top end of Hockerill Street, Bishop's Stortford. The top view shows the former Crown Inn when in use as a boys' school in 1897. Dating from the sixteenth century, it had a malthouse and brewery at the rear. Defoe had been a visitor and found it 'exceedingly good'. It closed in 1872 and became a boys' school in the 1890s, but was demolished in 1898. The lower view is a jettied house and shop on the other side of Hockerill Street next to the Red Lion.

Woodlands served as the manse for the Congregational church in Water Lane, Bishop's Stortford, in the 1870s. The Congregational church can just be glimpsed behind the tree on the other side of Water Lane in this view of about 1875. The old chapel, built in 1767, was too small for the growing congregation, who quickly raised the £2,500 construction costs. The minister in the 1870s was Rev William Cuthbertson. Standing on his lawn are Charles Portway and his family, together with Robert Lock, the draper. (Photograph by L. Bing)

The extraordinary Lululaund, Melbourne Road, Bushey, was designed for the portrait painter Sir Hubert von Herkomer by the American architect H.H. Richardson. Begun in 1886, it was completed in 1894, though Richardson died before the project was finished and Herkomer himself was responsible for much of the detail. The majority of the house was demolished in 1939, leaving only the entrance way, which survives as the entrance to a British Legion hall.

Potter Street, Bishop's Stortford, with decorations in place for the 1887 Golden Jubilee celebrations of the fiftieth anniversary of Queen Victoria's accession to the throne.

After the fire – what else but a sale? Robert Lock's salvage sale outside his badly burned Stortford House draper's shop in Potter Street, Bishop's Stortford, drew quite a crowd on Saturday 3 September 1887. The fire broke out on the evening of 5 August. Lock's family were got out safely, but in the course of the rescue the plate glass front windows were broken and the in-rush of air fanned the flames. Insurance covered the costs of the damage of what was said to be the largest of the town's shops. Lock went on to trade for at least another eight years, but had gone out of business by 1898.

High Street, Buntingford, from the junction with Baldock Road in 1949. Buntingford has been a market town since 1360, but grew as a settlement where Ermine Street crossed the River Rib. The Black Bull, on the right, may date back to the 1630s. Opposite is another former pub, the Indian Star, which has become a barber's shop!

A haycart comes up Station Road, Buntingford, in the late 1940s. The thatched Adam and Eve public house is now the site of a garage. It once boasted a pictorial inn sign, much to the disgust of some contemporary local residents.

The Eleanor Cross at Waltham Cross, as painted by Michael 'Angelo' Rooker, *c.* 1780. The cross is one of three of the original twelve erected in the 1290s to mark the resting places of the body of Edward I's Queen Eleanor as her corpse was carried towards London. The Waltham Cross was put up on the road, rather than at the abbey on the Essex side of the border. Restored several times, the original now carries facsimile statues. Behind is the Four Swans Inn, a resting place for the occupants of the coach.

The cross and the Four Swans from outside the Falcon Hotel in June 1893. Today, only the pole across the street remains of the Four Swans and the cross is now dwarfed by a modern shopping centre.

The yard of the Crown, 119 High Street, Berkhamsted, in the 1890s, complete with caged birds and what look like house plants being given an airing. The building dates from the sixteenth century, but the Crown was first recorded as an inn in 1743. In recent years it has had a series of names and was 'Cheerleaders' in 1995.

Back Lane, Berkhamsted, looking south-east towards St Peter's Church. The upper parts of the tower were added in 1535–6. This view, by J.C. Buckler, dates from the 1840s, after the first restoration of 1820 but before two further Victorian alterations in 1866–8 and 1871. On the right is the rear of the One Bell public house, which survived until 1959. Just visible in the right-hand corner is part of the Market House, an open timber-framed structure, that survived local attempts to demolish it but not a fire of 1854. The gabled house facing it on Back Lane, later a shop, was demolished to build the Court Theatre in 1916 and is now the site of a supermarket.

The Eight Bells on the corner of Park Street and Fore Street, Hatfield, about 1900. The pub featured in Charles Dickens' *Oliver Twist*, providing a stopping place for Bill Sykes after the murder of his girlfriend Nancy. The Eight Bells originally had only five bells to its name when first recorded in 1732, gaining the extra three in the mid-eighteenth century.

Flags are out in Fore Street, Hatfield, almost covering the shops and houses, for the visit of King Edward VII and Queen Alexandra in 1909. On the left is George Steabben's butcher's shop. Fore Street is largely Georgian, but owes some of its present appearance to the restoration work of local resident F.W. Speight between 1910 and 1930. (Photograph by William H. Cox)

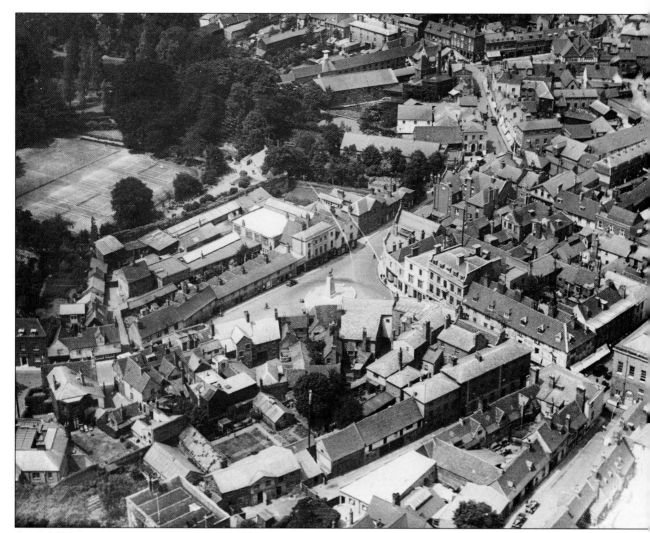

An aerial view of the western side of Hertford in the 1930s. In the centre is Parliament Square, created in 1922 when the war memorial was built and Parliament Row demolished. Mill Bridge runs northwards and to the west are the castle grounds, with Bell Lane and Church Street in the foreground. One corner of the Shire Hall is just visible. Hertford was one of five towns in the county mentioned in Domesday, owing its name and position to a ford just downstream from the bridge. Although the ring road has cut round the south side of the town many of the buildings in this view survive today.

Opposite: Fore Street and the Corn Exchange, Hertford, of 1857, a building Nikolaus Pevsner compared to an ambitious Methodist chapel. Beyond, on the corner of Market Place, is James Adam's Shire Hall of 1768–9. Fitton the chemist had moved from 37 Fore Street to No. 49 by 1898, having become chemist to Haileybury College and gone into retailing his own brand of mineral water. Market Street, which joins Fore Street just beyond the Corn Exchange, was cut through the site of the former town gaol. An earlier Corn Exchange and the Cross Keys Inn were demolished for the 1857 exchange, which had its urns and figure removed from the roof for safety during the Second World War.

Thomas Rowlandson's view of Hertford Market Place, *c*. 1800. Hertford's market days were Thursdays and Saturdays. Competition from Ware was seen off in the charter of 1441, which banned markets within a 7 mile radius from being held on those days. The open market moved from this site to Market Street in 1890 and later to a site on Butchery Green, though after the creation of the ring road stalls have returned to the streets behind the Shire Hall. (From an original in Hertford Museum)

The back garden of 25 Castle Street, Hertford, next to the Grammar School, photographed by R. Hallam on 10 September 1889. The occupant was Robert Thornton Andrews, an architect and surveyor who had his offices in Railway Street, adjoining the family business, which was a diverse operation encompassing timber, slate, saw mill and barges.

Balls Park lies to the south-west of Hertford town. Believed to date from the 1640s, it is more likely that the bulk of the house dates from 1705–25 when the sons of Sir John Harrison presided over substantial alterations. Until the mid-1880s it was owned by the Townshend family, but the 5th Marquis got into financial difficulty and let it to Sir George Faudel Phillips. This view from the 1870s shows the formal garden layout with new planting; the gardens were later altered by the Faudel Phillips family. The house was taken over by the local College of Education in 1947 and is now used by part of the University of Hertfordshire.

Hobletts Manor, High Street Green, Adeyfield, Hemel Hempstead. The top view shows the property from the road, the lower one the living rooms in 1928. Hobletts then belonged to Francis Cunningham, having been converted from two sixteenth-century cottages. It was not a manor house, and had been called Hobletts Orchard in 1898. Adeyfield formed one of the new neighbourhoods for the new town, grafted on to Hemel Hempstead from 1949, but Hobletts was to survive until 1965 when it was demolished for a development of twenty-nine houses built by C.T. Crouch.

St Mary's Church, Hitchin, *c.* 1908, from Market Place. The embattled tower was begun in the twelfth century and finished in the thirteenth, a symbol of local medieval wealth. Shipley Slipper was a peripatetic dentist, spending every other Tuesday at Hitchin and every other Thursday at Bishop's Stortford as part of a wider practice that he started around 1902. Ebenezer Allsop's hosier's shop was at No. 9 Market Place from about 1907.

The interior of Hitchin's Corn Exchange, a lithograph by the architect William Beck, probably produced before construction was finished in 1851. In operation the exchange had four rows of double-sided desks for the grain dealers to conduct their business. It opened in 1853, but undoubtedly it was the GNR railway line of 1850 that made it a financial success.

Berkhamsted's former Bridewell stood on the corner of the High Street and Cocks Lane or Bridewell (now Kings Road) and was photographed shortly before demolition in the early 1890s. It had been bought by the town in 1763. The presence of the policeman is fortuitous – since the town's present police station now stands on the site.

Leys Avenue, Letchworth. A Frith view of about 1929. Ebenezer Howard had originally intended to create a shopping company, as was later adopted at Welwyn Garden City, but in the event retailers took leases on shops on an individual basis. Leys Avenue was begun in 1907 and was given a subtle curve to break the straight lines of conventional shopping parades. This view was taken from the Norton Way South end looking west. Shops on the south side were designed by Bennet and Bidewell, again with the intention of variety. However, flowerbeds in front of the parades were quickly abandoned.

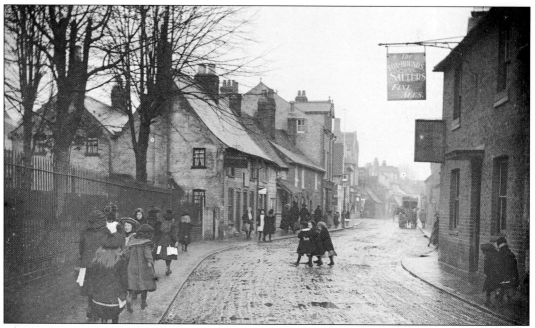

A very wintry day in Rickmansworth High Street about 1906, with girls on their way to the Parsonage Road school, behind the railings on the left. This had been built in 1854 for infants, but was enlarged in 1871 and took girls up to the age of fourteen. The double-bayed house just beyond dates from the seventeenth century. On the opposite side of the road is the Fox and Hounds public house, whose building dates from the seventeenth century but was refaced with stock bricks in the nineteenth century.

High Street, Royston, from the Cross on Saturday 5 June 1926, with Don Beale's confectionery shop and café on the corner. This junction on the A10 was very dangerous and there were a number of accidents in the 1920s. Road widening in 1927–8 resulted in the demolition of the former Crown Inn and Prince Charles Lodgings (an early seventeenth-century house) behind which the photographer was standing, but the accidents did not diminish. A petition for traffic lights in 1937 attracted nearly 2,000 signatures, but without result. After a bad crash between two lorries in 1938, lights were installed at last in 1940 – but covered because of the blackout!

Market Place, St Albans, a water-colour by G. Shepherd, 1812. The Clock Tower in the centre of the view was built in 1403–12 and substantially restored by Sir George Gilbert Scott in 1866, though it retained shops at its base into the 1890s. The open-sided structure covered a pump and was on the site of the Market Cross, which had been demolished in 1810 after a wagoner collided with it. The two buildings alongside the tower are now Nos 1–2 Market Place and are both timber-framed buildings dating from the seventeenth century. The brick building alongside survived into the twentieth century but has now been replaced by a 1930s Georgian-style shop building.

The Town Hall and Market Place, St Albans, an early morning view, *c.* 1900. St Albans Town Hall was designed by George Smith and opened in 1831, replacing the former Town Hall, which stood on the corner of Upper Dagnall Street and Market Place. It served as a seat for both the corporation and the magistrates, and disagreements between the two had delayed selection of a suitable site. Smith received the freedom of the borough for his efforts, although the costs reduced the money available for mayoral feasting for a full six years!

Swiss Cottage, Cassiobury Park, Watford, *c.* 1900. Swiss Cottage was by the River Gade and was intended for picnics and open-air functions. It survived the demolition of Cassiobury House, but was burned out in an accidental fire in the Second World War.

High Street and the former Town Hall, Ware, 1899. Ware had two 'town hall' buildings. This one, built in 1827 and funded by public subscription, was originally arcaded to provide a cornmarket below and assembly rooms above, but it could not compete with Hertford and was sold; shops took over the ground floor. Augustus Wilkinson was the landlord of the Lion and Wheatsheaf in 1898, which has become one of Ware's lost pubs.

Opposite: High Street, Watford, in the early 1890s. The gabled building on the right beyond the Rose and Crown is Francis Fisher's new butcher's shop, completed in 1888. Market Place has been cut through between the Rose and Crown and the Compasses, and the former has been altered. On market days the right-hand side of the street would have been crowded with animal pens. Redevelopment has claimed the majority of buildings in this view including the Rose and Crown, demolished in 1968.

No. 84 High Street, Ware, 1899. No. 84, which was built as a hall house in the fifteenth century and was considerably altered in the seventeenth century, stands on an island site and survives today. Beyond it on West Street is Ware's second Town Hall, in use as such from 1867 and run by The Old Town Hall Syndicate until the 1940s. The Town Hall building dates from the early eighteenth century, but was probably refronted at the beginning of the nineteenth century.

A trailer with a Wickham railcar tries to negotiate the streets by Ware Bridge in the early 1950s. Wickham's had been founded in 1886 as a motorcar and general engineering business by Denis Wickham but focused on making rail motor trolleys in 1922, adding diesel railcars from 1926, and exporting to many parts of the world. The business was taken over in 1987 and the Ware factory closed in 1991.

From small beginnings: Barclays' first branch at Bridge Road, Welwyn Garden City, c. 1925. The Midland Bank had loaned the Garden City company the money to buy the Panshanger estate on which the new town was built, and took advantage of its investment to open the first bank branch in the town early in 1922; Barclays followed a few months later. Lloyds joined the fray with another wooden hut in 1929, but in the same year Barclays acquired more dignified premises in Howardsgate.

Handside Lane, Welwyn Garden City, 1927 – publicity photograph to emphasise what the new town had to offer. Welwyn Garden City was founded in 1920 by a private company run by Ebenezer Howard and the principal architects were Louis de Soissons and Arthur W. Kenyon. These houses in Handside Lane were among the first to be built in 1920, designed by C.M. Crichmer; residents in the road included Howard himself. Mud was a problem for the early residents who, according to a *Punch* cartoon of 1924, needed wellington boots to get to the station – and left them there ready for the trip home at night.

Brockswood Lane, Welwyn Garden City, c. 1927. Construction of houses in Brockswood Lane was under way only two to three weeks after work had begun in Handside Lane, and here too the mud proved to be a considerable obstacle for the first incoming families. One family, who moved in to No. 8 in January 1921, had to do without their furniture on the first night as the removal lorry got stuck in the lane's mud. The following day it was unloaded into the nearest empty house and the town's narrow gauge railway had to be used to get it to Brockswood Lane.

POVERTY AND CHARITY

A boy band, with child inmates and staff outside the front door of Hitchin Workhouse, *c.* 1880. The administration of the poor law had been a parochial responsibility until 1834, when unions of parishes were set up. Hitchin joined a union of twenty-six other parishes, and its overcrowded workhouse at the corner of Tilehouse Street and Maltmill Lane was replaced by a new establishment at Chalkdell, opened on 16 January 1837, and enlarged in 1886. The workhouse had its own infirmary and when the workhouse system ended it became an annexe to the Lister Hospital, used for the chronically sick and for older people.

Class group in the National Refugees Home for Boys and Girls, Royston, shortly after the home opened in 1908. The new building stood at the top of Barkway Road and was intended for homeless and destitute children, though the initial intake was girls only, as in this view – some girls have closely cut hair. The home was later known as the Shaftsbury House School.

Hertford Union Workhouse, Ware Road – a Charles Martin postcard of *c*. 1910. Hertford's workhouse had new buildings constructed in 1867–70, though not without squabbles between architect Frederick Peck and the quantity surveyor, and when the work was completed in 1870 the doors proved to be a very poor fit. The workhouse remained in use until 1919, when the remaining inmates were transferred to Ware and the buildings became Kingsmead School, for children who, in the language of the time, were 'mentally defective'.

ARRIVAL OF THE PRINCE AND PRINCESS OF WALES TO LAY THE FOUNDATION-STONE OF THE ORPHAN ASYLUM AT WATFORD.—SEE NEXT PAGE.

The London Orphan Asylum was founded in 1813 by philanthropist Andrew Reed and was based in Lower Clapton Road, Hackney, from 1820 to 1871. With the development of the area and following a typhus outbreak in 1866, the governors of the asylum decided to move out of London. They acquired a site just to the west of Watford Junction station. The top view shows the arrival of the Prince and Princess of Wales to lay the foundation stone for the new site. Children sang, a band played and a short service was followed by a repast. The lower view shows the intended layout of the new asylum by architect Henry Dawson. The new buildings were completed in 1871 and remained in use as a school until 1939 when the children were evacuated, never to return.

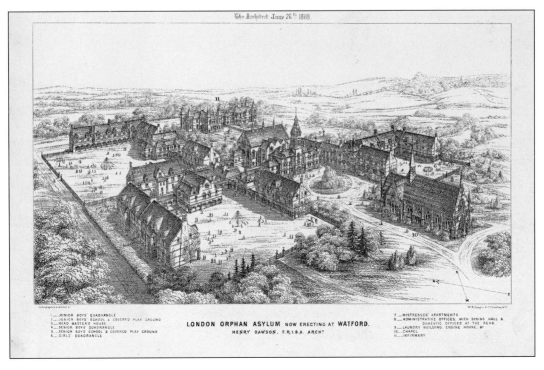

The Architect June 26th 1869.

1.—JUNIOR BOYS' QUADRANGLE
2.—JUNIOR BOYS' SCHOOL & COVERED PLAY GROUND
3.—HEAD MASTER'S HOUSE
4.—SENIOR BOYS' QUADRANGLE
5.—SENIOR BOYS' SCHOOL & COVERED PLAY GROUND
6.—GIRLS' QUADRANGLE

7.—MISTRESSES' APARTMENTS
8.—ADMINISTRATIVE OFFICES, WITH DINING HALL & DOMESTIC OFFICES AT THE REAR
9.—LAUNDRY BUILDING, ENGINE HOUSE, &c
10.—CHAPEL
11.—INFIRMARY

LONDON ORPHAN ASYLUM NOW ERECTING AT WATFORD.
HENRY DAWSON, F.R.I.B.A. ARCHT

Cottage at Watford, 1867. By contrast, this was the sort of housing that many of the rural poor would have had to put up with. The tubs and mangle suggest that the inhabitants may have taken in washing to make ends meet. The location of this view is not recorded; it could have been on one of the lanes branching off from the High Street or north of the town.

The Booksellers' Provident Retreat, Abbots Langley, shortly after opening in 1845. The Retreat was the creation of the Booksellers' Provident Society on 3½ acres donated by paper manufacturer John Dickinson. The building was designed by W.H. Cooper and was intended for those members of the society receiving annuities, or their widows. The main site had bungalows added in 1965 and the original almshouse building, named Dickinson House in September 1979, now houses seven flats and the Society's library.

The former Hoddesdon Workhouse in 1866. From 1570 this had been the Dolphin public house; it was then leased to the parish to serve as a workhouse from 1757 to 1833, when it again reverted to serving ale, this time as the Five Horseshoes until demolition shortly after this view was taken.

Cherry Tree Yard, Amwell End, Ware, 1936. Small yards and courts provided housing for the poor in towns; this group of cottages was close to the river at the rear of the public house the yard was named after. The six yards on the east side of Amwell End were identified as having poor sanitation as early as 1849, but it took the initiative of Ware Urban District Council surveyor Robert Grantham in the 1930s to begin the process of slum clearance, which even then was not completed until after 1945.

Butchery Green, Hertford, *c.* 1927. The weatherboarded eighteenth-century houses were part of a neighbourhood whose inhabitants had determined elections to the pre-1832 unreformed Hertford Corporation. It was described at the time as 'a low and grimy quarter of the town, [where] bargemen, tramps, rag bottle gatherers and people whose means of livelihood were as dubious as their characters congregated'. The area ultimately formed the site of the open market and is now re-named as part of the Bircheley Green shopping centre.

SHOPS, MARKETS AND
PUBLIC HOUSES

Baldock market on the High Street about 1926. Baldock's original weekly market dated back to the Templars' charter of 1217 and was held on Saturdays. This was altered to Wednesdays and then in 1566 to Thursday after a local petition. It changed again to Fridays in 1807 but then gradually ceased to be held. A revival of a livestock market on Thursdays in 1883 lasted only a year and it was not until 1925 that a livestock market was successfully revived, this time on Saturdays as none of the previous changes of day had been given any legal validity. Poultry, eggs, cattle and agricultural implements were sold and there were auctions. The market succeeded this time, until the disruption of the Second World War.

Boff Davis in the doorway of his tiny confectioner's shop, Station Road, Harpenden, *c.* 1885. The door on the left led to a cobbler's shop kept by J. Davies. Successive road repairs had left the cottage floor 8 inches below the road level – which must have made both shops damp. The cottage was demolished in the early 1890s and replaced by a butcher's shop.

Thomas Franklin's butcher's shop, 5 Potter Street, Bishop's Stortford, about 1902. The public health concerns of the late nineteenth century did not extend to the open display of meat outside shops – after all how else was the butcher to display his wares?

Hoddesdon's market in the High Street, *c.* 1920. Like Baldock, Hoddesdon had had a traditional market, but after the removal of the Market House in 1833 it had gradually ceased to function. Following the initiative of a local auctioneer, a new livestock market opened on 24 March 1886 and was then held each Wednesday. After the First World War the livestock element became less popular and eventually the rights to the market were acquired from the Marquis of Salisbury. Livestock pens were replaced by covered stalls, which were congregated round the Clock Tower.

H.P. Tyler's boot and shoe emporium, High Street, Rickmansworth, in 1912. Tyler's had taken over the Ward family business around 1906. John Ward had founded the shop in 1830, living with his family on the premises and building workshops to make boots in the yard at the back. Tyler's was to last until 1966, when the shop was demolished.

One of the small shops in Shenley Road, Borehamwood, was H. Starck's confectionery and tobacconist's shop. In the Parade, and standing at the corner with Furzehill Road, Starck's business lasted from shortly before 1908 to the early 1920s.

Have motor, will travel. Alfred J. Miller and his van in the 1920s. The motor van made it much easier for small rural businesses to deliver to their customers. Miller's business at Braughing had been founded around 1909 and lasted into the early 1930s.

However, before the First World War the horse and cart reigned supreme. Mr Frederick William Pavey and his boy stand outside Pavey's baker's shop at 54 Musley Hill, Ware, about 1910. Pavey had been in business for about five years and was still there in 1914, but the shop had closed by 1917.

The Brown family pose outside their family grocery business at 2 Dunmow Road, Bishop's Stortford, in 1891. Ebenezer Brown had set up the shop in the mid-1880s, and it had passed to William Brown, who had also become the local sub-postmaster, by the early 1920s. The Browns kept the shop on until 1968 and then moved round the corner to 6 London Road.

After Lock's drapery business closed in the mid-1890s, the shop at 93 Potter Street, Bishop's Stortford, passed through a variety of hands. In 1908 it was divided between a wool shop and a servants' registry office. Almost all the women are holding knitting needles and wool – but were they all wool shop employees?

Ironmonger's on the corner. Ridley and Son's shop, Station Road, Harpenden, summer *c.* 1905. Billy Ridley's shop was one of only four in Station Road before the First World War and delivered paraffin oil by horse and cart all over Harpenden and the neighbouring villages. The shop later became a bank.

Annie Turner and local postmen outside her sub-post office at 57 High Street, Kings Langley, in the 1890s. The post office had been established in 1889 in a cottage that had served as the parish workhouse from 1750 until the abolition of direct parochial poor relief in 1834. In 1908 the Post Office provided a purpose-built building at 45 High Street, which closed in 1970.

Welwyn Garden City Stores opened in October 1921, on the site of the later Roseanne House. The top view shows the warehouse building. Inside there were a number of separate 'departments'; the lower view shows the hardware section, which opened a few months after the food departments. There was a fire in 1924, which damaged but did not destroy the building. The shop was intended to be a social centre and even had its own crèche. A bad trading year in 1927 led to the abandonment of a home delivery service and cuts in staff wages but eventually the store moved to a new building on Parkway in 1933 (where the John Lewis store is today) and the old premises were demolished in 1939.

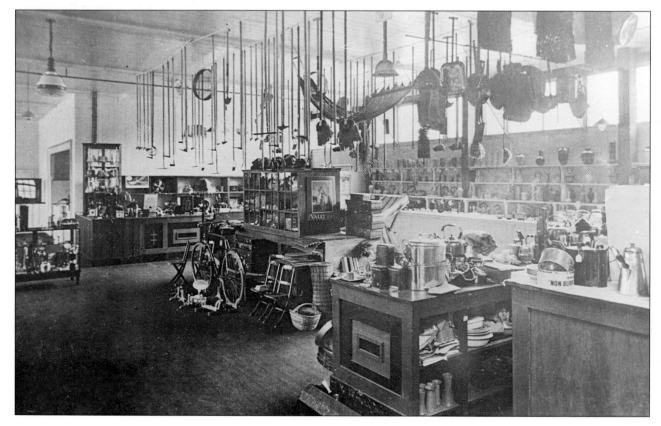

The Jolly Miller and adjoining tobacconist's shop at 5 High Street, Kings Langley, about 1906, when the licensee was Albert Smith. Smith's predecessor, Francis Wood, may have been responsible for setting up the joint business, since he is also listed as beer retailer and tobacconist in the 1902 county directory. The Jolly Miller was traditionally a carters' pub, providing ale for those taking straw to London. It ceased to be a pub in 1919 but the building still survives.

Buckland's post office, on the west side of the village street, had once been the Chequers Inn, run by the Beale family from 1814–54. Alongside, in this mid-1920s view, is the thatched Coffee Tavern and beyond the junction with Whiteleys Lane is the shop that probably belonged to Joseph Carter in the early 1920s. The Chequers was still marked as a pub on the 1923 Ordnance Survey map.

The Cow Roast Hotel, Wigginton, around 1910, when Walter Thomas Chandler was the landlord. The pub was a halting place on the drovers' road from the Midlands and North Wales and was originally the Cow and later – rather more appropriately – the Cow Rest, though it had gained its present name by 1851. It was a popular place for local excursions. Chandler arrived around 1909 and had gone by 1914.

The Silver Cup Inn on the St Albans Road, Harpenden, *c.* 1900. The Silver Cup was built in 1838 by a Wheathampstead brewer. The licensee was Richard Archer, who poses with his family. John Carter had kept the pub before, but the Archer connection had been broken by 1902. The Silver Cup pond on the common opposite was filled in in the 1960s. The part of the pub at the rear has lost a storey and there have been some minor changes to the windows but otherwise it remains unchanged today.

Water End in North Mimms parish has two adjacent pubs. This is The Old Maypole and the adjoining smithy at the turn of the century. A house on the site of the pub was recorded as newly built in 1716 and had become a pub by 1756. Divided into two in 1797, one part was demolished shortly afterwards. The pub was held by the Massey family from 1822–99, who also leased the field behind the Woodman public house.

The Woodman, Water End, c. 1906. First recorded as a beerhouse in 1843 the Woodman was acquired by a Hatfield brewer in 1851, who sold it to Pryor Reid of Hatfield in 1888. Landlords in the 1880s and 1890s also featured as shop keepers – just as the Massey family doubled up as blacksmiths.

The Fighting Cocks, Abbey Mill Lane, St Albans, *c.* 1890. Built on medieval foundations that may once have been a turret or back gate in the walls of St Albans Abbey, the pub was rebuilt after a flood in 1600 and was known as the Round House until the nineteenth century. There had once been a cockpit attached and it can still be seen in a part of the bar that is lower than the rest. In 1855 it had become the Fisherman beerhouse, suggesting a period without a licence, but it had regained a full licence by the 1890s and was vying for trade, claiming to be the oldest inhabited house in England!

Landlord Peter Messider (standing in the doorway), family and customers outside the Valiant Trooper, Trooper Road, Aldbury, around 1925. From left to right: Frederick William Delderfield, Levi Collier, Mrs Delderfield, Arthur Delderfield, Ada Messider (Peter's daughter) and Reg Welling. The pub dates from 1752 and was originally the Royal Oak, becoming the Trooper in 1791, with 'Valiant' added in 1890. The pub had an unusual customer at Christmas times in the 1920s – one local woman used to go in dressed up in her husband's clothes, which were several times too large for her. But she never took a drink!

The Bull Inn, Whitwell, a Buckler drawing of about 1835. The Bull was already an established inn in 1675 and may date back to medieval times. The building in this view dates from the early seventeenth century. Licensees would have done well out of Whitwell Statute Fair at the end of September; one diarist wrote in 1808 that he dined in a company of twenty on beef, chicken, ham, goose, duck and pie, at 15 shillings each – which he regarded as his most expensive statute dinner to date.

The Black Horse, Dog Kennel Lane, Chorleywood, about 1900. In existence as the Earl of Winchelsea's Arms in 1772 and later the Finch's Arms, the pub moved to this site after the coming of the railway to Chorleywood in 1890, as the Gilliats, lord and lady of the manor, had had enough of the navvies who had built the railway using the old pub on their land. So the licence transferred to an existing house on the edge of the common and the pub reverted to its earlier name, the Black Horse.

Time had already been called at the Dog's Head in the Pot, Fishmarket, Bishop's Stortford, in 1894. A. Maxwell took the photograph (as the building was 'in the process of obliteration') as a commission from local builder and historian John Laybank Glasscock (1854–1929), who worked as an architect for Benskins Brewery and supervised the rebuilding of many old pubs. Glasscock recorded: 'I had this view taken in order to shew how this old timber framed house might have been easily restored and its original character and style preserved.' But it was not to be. Directories only list the pub as the Dog so perhaps Glasscock was recording its unofficial name, something to rival modern fictitious combinations like the Rat and Carrot. Time for a revival?

A TOUCH OF RELIGION

St Albans Cathedral, in a view looking south, with the newly restored west end gleaming very white in the sunlight, suggesting that this photograph, possibly by T.M. Cooper, was taken in the early 1880s. Below are the backs of houses in Fishpool Street and to the left is Romeland House, attributed to Edward Strong, Christopher Wren's master mason, who died in 1723. The former abbey church was in a poor state of repair in the early nineteenth century and the west front was ruinous. Major restoration work was begun under Sir George Gilbert Scott but stopped after his death in 1878, and it was only with the intervention of Lord Grimthorpe, who directed and funded the project, that it was completed. To the west of the cathedral and rising above the houses is the Gatehouse of the 1360s.

The former Old Church of Flaunden was still extant when drawn by Henry Munroe and engraved by W.B. Cooke in 1815, though it appeared to be more farm building than place of worship. The thirteenth-century church incorporated a priest's house at one end and a timber-framed tower. Replaced as the village church in 1838, it gradually disintegrated although the ruins still had visible traces of thirteenth-century wall paintings. Nothing now remains but a few fragments of wall.

All Saints' Church, Hertford, drawn by W.H. Taylor and reproduced as a lithograph in 1849. There had been a church on this site in 1086, but it was largely rebuilt in the fifteenth century. During the early morning of 22 December 1891 a flue overheated and started a fire that destroyed the church. Luckily the plate had been removed from the church and the records, stored in a chest, survived the blaze. The present church was completed in 1893, with a tower added in 1905. It is now separated from the town by the ring road.

St Mary's Church, Therfield, had been in a poor state in 1664 and repaired, but when John Goodwin Hale became rector in 1874 he found the chancel was unsafe, the seventeenth-century plaster ceiling close to collapse and parts of the walls sinking into a former moat that lay below the church. He decided to have the church rebuilt. A temporary brick church was built nearby and the rebuilding supervised by architect G.E. Pritchet, who retained only the chancel, the north and south windows and the double piscina from the old church. Both views were taken at the start of the work in 1874. The upper shows the poor state of the church and the lower view captures the workforce with the rector. What appears to be part of the former church clock lies in the foreground.

Oxhey Chapel was built in 1612 by Sir James Altham as a place of worship for his nearby house, St Cleeres (later Oxhey Place). The chapel seated forty and its reredos may have come from the original Oxhey Place when it was demolished in 1688. Both views date from the 1890s when the chapel was still surrounded by park land. Subsequently it was restored, losing its gabled roof and dormer and the surrounding trees. It survives today but a housing estate has replaced the park land.

Bell ringing at St Leonard's Church, Flamstead, 1952. St Leonard's has a Norman tower and nave, whose patched brick work includes some Roman examples. One of the county's best series of medieval wall paintings was uncovered here in the 1920s, with further discoveries made in 1974.

St Cecilia's Church porch, Little Hadham, photographed by W. Minet in 1903. The porch is late medieval and its wide open sides made it perfect for a photographic pose. The tower dates from about 1400 and within there remains one of the county's few surviving three-decker pulpits, dated 1633.

Consecration service for St Paul's Church, Chipperfield, 1837. Artist George Hawkins has taken the original sketch by the church's architect, Thomas Talbot Bury, and added figures for his lithograph of the consecration service. Chipperfield was part of Kings Langley parish and the new church did not become a parish church until 1848. The costs of the new church were met by subscription, the surplus going to an endowment fund. The church faced rivalry from the local Baptist community, strong in the area since the 1690s, and a new Baptist chapel was also completed in 1837.

Churches were important centres for local social life. This fete was held on the lawn of the rectory of St Andrew's Church, Hertford, in June 1902. The fete may have been planned to coincide with the coronation of Edward VII, but this was delayed by the king's serious illness. The rector at the time was Evan Killin Roberts.

Some Nonconformist churches were wealthy purpose-built structures; others were less well endowed. Mrs Humphrey is sweeping the steps of the Primitive Methodist chapel, Solesbridge Lane, Chorleywood, in the 1890s. The chapel had once been used by Quakers and was demolished about 1895 after the congregation had moved to a new chapel at Colleywood.

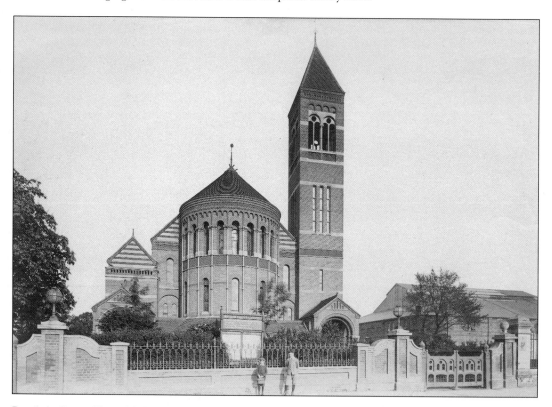

Beechen Grove Chapel, Watford, *c.* 1900. Watford's Baptist community had expanded in numbers in the nineteenth century. The original church was replaced by this one, designed by J. Wallis Chapman between 1876–8. The curved apse and partially detached campanile brought a touch of Italy to the Watford skyline.

WAR, LAW AND LOCAL GOVERNMENT

A service was held at Hartham, Hertford, for the homecoming of the Herts Militia from the Boer War in 1902. The Marquis of Salisbury, one of those on the platform behind the clerics, presented each soldier with a silver tobacco box after the service.

Soldiers, possibly part of The County of London Battalion, are greeted by crowds at Watford Junction station as they march down Station Road to a review at St Albans. There were a great deal of troop manoeuvres in the early days of the war and two inspections of forces at St Albans in September 1914, one by the King and one by Lord Kitchener on 18 and 22 September respectively. The photograph may have been taken by Frederick Downer, who was very active in recording Watford life during the early years of the First World War.

Soldiers on parade at the start of the visit of the Prince and Princess of Wales to Hertford on 23 July 1906, which began at the station at Cowbridge. The Prince was to open new school buildings at Christ's Hospital School. Founded in the City of London in 1546, and with links with Hertford that dated back to the seventeenth century, the girls' school had joined the boys' at Hertford in 1778. The move of the boys' school to Horsham in 1902 enabled the expansion to take place.

The downing of a Zeppelin, which crashed near Cuffley on 3 September 1916, caused intense excitement locally. The airship caught fire in mid-air after being strafed by Lt W.L. Robinson. There were no survivors from the blaze, which was visible 16 miles away. Local roads were packed with traffic as people tried to get to the scene. The view of a little local traffic difficulty was taken on 'Zeppelin Sunday'. The lower view shows Lt Robinson, who was later awarded a VC, and soldiers with parts of the wreckage. Many pieces of the Zeppelin were taken away as souvenirs – and there can be few local museums that do not have their own unique bit of the airship.

St Albans prepares for war. The top view shows soldiers in Clarence Park and the bottom a column in Hatfield Road near St Peter's Street.

The 7th Battalion of the Cheshire Regiment on parade in Baldock High Street in 1915. The first contingent of soldiers to be billeted with local people at Baldock arrived two days after the war started in August 1914. The Cheshire Regiment was sent out to Gallipoli and suffered heavy casualties. Other troops who passed through the town included Australians and South Africans. The South Africans were there during a snow blizzard and built an enormous snowman in the High Street.

A horse-drawn Red Cross ambulance with nurses and staff outside the walls of Hatfield House during the Boer War. The Red Cross opened a hospital in Hatfield in January 1916, which lasted until February 1919, and during the Second World War Hatfield House itself served as a military hospital.

During the First World War part of Napsbury Hospital at London Colney became the County of Middlesex War Hospital. This view shows the dispensary, *c*. 1916. Napsbury Manor Farm had been bought by the London County Council to build an additional lunatic asylum, which opened in 1905. After the war the military hospital closed and Napsbury remained in use until the early 1980s for people with mental illness or learning difficulties.

Digswell House, Welwyn Garden City, had been built for Lord Cowper around 1807. During the First World War it was taken over as a hospital. This undated view shows Australian officers who had lost limbs taking part in a 'golf stable'.

Mechanisation of a kind. Troops from The 2nd London Division and their bicycles line up in the village street at Redbourn around 1914. The view featured as a postcard and was sent by a local girl, 'Lily', to a friend at Hither Farm at Thorley. 'Very quiet here without the soldiers,' she commented, 'they kept us busy.'

Soldiers from The 2nd North Midland Brigade march out of Markyate along the Pickford Road in 1915, passing St John's Church Hall (with the steeple) at the bottom of the hill. Many regiments were successively stationed at Markyate and for much of the war the former Sun Inn on the High Street was used as an HQ. The YMCA put up a large wooden recreation hut for soldiers on the south side of Pickford Road further up the hill. Some soldiers were camped outside the town, others billeted with local families and some married local girls.

The home front in another war. Here troops on a visit to Murphy Radio's factory in Welwyn Garden City are getting better acquainted with one of the workers. From humble beginnings in 1928, Frank Murphy's business had grown so that by 1939 it was one of the six largest British radio manufacturers. After the outbreak of war the plant took on a range of government contracts. Radio production resumed in 1945 and lasted until 1964, two years after a take-over by Rank Industries.

Wartime hospitality at its best at Flamstead as Boy Scouts bring out the barrel, not too far distant from the local pub.

Watford took government warnings of gas attacks very seriously and was determined to preserve everyone. What a dog's sensitive nose made of the inside of a rubber gas mask is not on record.

One of the many airfields round London was at Panshanger outside Welwyn Garden City. A Tiger Moth and pilot stand on the field. Panshanger was constructed as a 'dummy' airfield on land owned by Lord Desborough, and as such was intended to entice German bombers away from the de Havilland aircraft works at Hatfield. It was later used in the development of the Mosquito aircraft.

The Ware fire brigade poses with its gleaming horse-drawn engine at Buryfield in 1912. At the time, the engine was stored in a building in Church Street and in the event of a fire the horses had to be rounded up from Buryfield and Crane Mead. The first Ware brigade was founded by an insurance company as a response to the danger posed by the town's timber-framed buildings and maltings. It was reorganised in 1889 and came under the control of the Urban District Council in 1898. The steam engine in this view was bought in 1907, the year after a disastrous fire at Victoria Maltings.

It would have taken many horse-drawn engines some time to reach a fire and it looks as if the efforts of the Hatfield crew at Woodhall Farm in 1889 had not been enough to prevent substantial damage. Horse-drawn engines could not reach fires quickly, and sometimes had accidents attempting to do so. The original Woodhall house had suffered the same misfortune as the farm, burning down in 1792. The Hatfield brigade got a new Shand Mason pump in 1909 but back in 1889, after best efforts had been made, there was nothing more to do than pose on the rooftop for a great picture.

A terminal fire at the Fox and Hounds in Barley at the end of August 1950 destroyed the pub, which had been first recorded as the Swan in 1670. It had changed its name and acquired the gallows sign across the road in the 1820s. The sign and the name were transferred to another Barley pub, the former Waggon and Horses, in 1955.

The aftermath of an explosion at Two Waters Mill on 19 November 1918. The Patent Degreasing Manufacturing Co. had taken over from the Rigill Manufacturing Co. around 1912. The mill had been used to make a petrol substitute, artificial and carbon bisulphide used in removing fat from wool. The twenty employees had smelt fumes and escaped before the blast, at just before 10 a.m., so there was no loss of life, but the force of the blast destroyed the mill and started a huge blaze that was put out by engines from Hemel Hempstead and from Dickinson's own Apsley Mill brigade. Surrounding houses were bombarded by metal and masonry, while Paxton's Furniture next to the mill was completely destroyed.

The famous lock-up at Shenley, photographed by G.L. Blake one late spring day about 1950. Almost buried under the flowering horse chestnut tree, the lock-up was looking a little worn after the war years. Dating from the eighteenth century it was repaired around 1810. Each of the small barred windows has a suitable injunction on the lintel: 'Be sober', 'Do well', 'Fear not' and 'Be vigilant'.

A battle was in progress over rights of way at Piggott's Hill, Harpenden, on 7 December 1913. Those who objected to the blockage, led by Spencer Pickering, have just crossed the fences ready to remove the obstructions. But on their return on the following Sunday they found the fences had been put back up and liberally smeared with tar. Pickering was able to suggest that the landowner be given seven days' grace to settle the matter before it went to court, and averted a further destruction of fences.

Police pose outside Hatfield's police station in the early 1860s. By the 1830s policing standards varied widely. Some towns had their own forces, some parishes retained rural constables; a sub-committee set up by the county's justices of the peace in 1839 found some parishes had no constables at all, while the force at Great Amwell had 'none but old Dogberries'. The committee's report led to the establishment of a county force in 1841.

The interior of Hertford's Crown Court in the Shire Hall in 1823, with the accused John Thurtle and Joseph Hunt about to plead in the case of the murder of William Weare. Weare and Thurtle were gamblers and fight promoters. After Weare cheated Thurtle out of £300 at cards, Thurtle and his accomplice Hunt invited him to a shooting weekend at Aldenham, during which they shot and bludgeoned him to death. After they were arrested Hunt turned King's evidence and the whole case attracted substantial national press coverage. When both were found guilty, Hunt was transported to Australia but Thurtle, still denying his involvement, was hanged outside Hertford Gaol in January 1824.

Perambulations of parish and borough boundaries were vital to medieval communities to ensure that markers had not been shifted by inhabitants of neighbouring parishes. By the eighteenth century they also afforded local people the chance for an entertaining day out – especially if there were any public houses on route. Hertford's town boundaries were perambulated on 18 September 1920. The top view shows the traditional bumping against a tree marking a boundary point. Usually a boy was used, with the intention that the bump fixed it in his memory especially if a long time ensued until the next perambulation. Rivers did not stop the perambulators, as the lower picture shows.

EVENTS AND PASTIMES

Winter delights. Tobogganing at Newberries Park, Radlett, 17 January 1926. Newberries had been so named by Robert Phillimore in the 1830s. After passing through several owners, the estate had been sold to George Mills in 1903. Mills took a positive attitude to local people enjoying his land, including Shenley Hill, so much so that the estate came to be known as Miller's Park. Miller got into financial difficulties and Newberries was sold in the 1930s. Part became a golf club for a time, part was built over, while the house itself, after use by an insurance company during the Second World War, was demolished in 1957.

All the fun of the Statute Fair at Markyate in 1913. By this date the autumn fair had moved to Hicks Lane; it had originally been held along the High Street and like many such fairs was the occasion for labourers to seek to hire themselves out for the coming twelve months.

The September Fair in preparation on Church Green, Harpenden, in the 1890s. It was held between similar fairs held at Hemel Hempstead and Stevenage. The small shops round the green included a wheelwright, a fishmonger, Hosky Jenning's tiny boot repair shop – whose low sill often provided a seat for the ancient 'Grandfather Sampson' – and a wine and beer retailer. Church Green has more trees today and Luton Road to the right is far busier.

The marriage of the vicar was a very special occasion. The triumphal arch was put up at Aldenham to celebrate the marriage of the Rev Kenneth Francis Gibbs to Mabel Alice Barnet on 5 June 1894. The groom was thirty-eight, the bride just nineteen. Gibbs was the third son of Henry Hucks Gibbs, 1st Lord Aldenham, who had bought the rights to present to the vicarage in 1877 and owned nearby Aldenham House, described as 'an opulent country retreat', so in one sense the wedding was a celebration for both squire and parson.

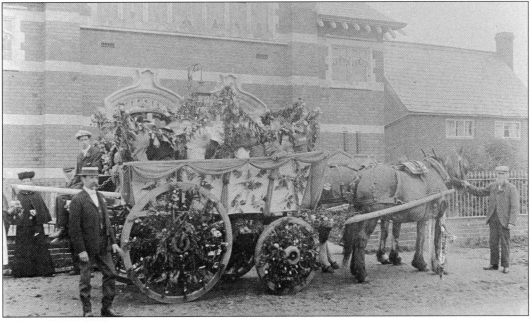

High jinks and festivities outside Breachwood Green Baptist chapel, Kings Walden, c. 1905. Mr Wilson is smartly dressed for the occasion in jacket and straw boater. Hertfordshire Archives would welcome any further information about this photograph, which was taken after the rebuilding of the chapel in 1904. The Baptists in the area had experienced something of a revival under the pastorship of G.D. Stapeley from 1880–9 and it was the growth of the congregation during the 1890s that prompted the need for larger premises.

New towns, old traditions. A May Day parade at Letchworth, with the pole in motion, 1909. The procession included representatives from local schools, the First Garden City Company, the parish council, estate workers and trades unions, and finished with the crowning of the May Queen. Such processions, fancy dress competitions and created days like 'Arbor Day' (for tree planting) formed an important part of the early life of the new garden city, and even the founder, Ebenezer Howard, dressed up for this one, if a little self consciously.

A bicycle parade at Rickmansworth enlivens a Bank Holiday on 26 August 1908. The cyclists are standing on the approach to the Metropolitan railway station.

Great Hormead combined with Little Hormead and Hare Street to welcome home native soldiers, sailors and airmen on 25 July 1919. Funded by local resident W.H. Evans, the day included a feast followed by a whist drive, shooting competitions and 'animal shooting'. The sports were held in a field at the top of Horseshoe Hill, where this photograph was taken. The day finished with tea and a dance.

Happy and Glorious. A dinner to celebrate the coronation of Edward VII in the Hertford Corn Exchange in 1902.

The West Hertfordshire Hospital Carnival at Hemel Hempstead on Saturday 19 July 1913 offered the chance for a fancy dress competition. Alfred and Elizabeth Pullum, as Professor Bunkum and assistant, did not manage the top prize, which went to another bicycle sporting a veritable bower of flowers on top of it, but at least their efforts were commended. The carnival was just part of a continuing campaign to raise funds for Hemel's local hospital.

Concert groups were very popular in the 1920s and 1930s. This is the Whitwell Magpies in full costume.

This parade on Melbourne Street, Royston, in 1924 was also part of a grand effort to replace the small cottage hospital with a larger one that would be capable of meeting the needs of the expanding town. A new hospital had first been proposed in 1922 and a site found on London Road. Fund-raising efforts included the raffling of a donkey by local butcher Bert Smoothy and were rounded off by the Grand Fete and Old English Fayre held over five days from 20 May 1924. There were stallholders in costume and the week raised £1,716, ensuring that building work could be completed. The hospital opened in August 1924. (Photograph by Robert H. Clark)

Fund-raising for the Red Cross at Barkway in October 1915. The group, which includes the vicar, Rev Wilfred Thomas Stubbs, is standing by the wall of Barkway House. Stubbs' wife Muriel is beside him. Their son James is behind the barrow, in a sun-hat, with sister Catherine, also in a hat, standing to his right. Emma Brown, who organised local milk deliveries, is standing by the horse and cart, loaned by T. Pigg and Miss Georgie Pigg, and George 'Stumpy' Watson is seated on the barrow. The cart was used to take fruit and vegetables to local villages during October, the sale of which contributed to funds that eventually totalled over £20.

The King is dead. Long live the King. The proclamation of George V outside St Peter and St Paul's Church, Tring, May 1910.

Excitement at North Mimms in September 1912. This Short S38 bi-plane of the Naval Wing of the Royal Flying Corps may have been taking part in army manoeuvres in East Anglia and, if so, was on route from Hendon or Farnborough to Thetford, when it dropped in on Hertfordshire.

There was less choice of where to land for this bi-plane, which crashed at Lye Hill, Breachwood Green, around 1905.

Lorries have gathered on Tring High Street by the war memorial during the Great Strike of 1926, preparing to deliver milk from Aylesbury Vale to London. As part of its support for the anti-strike action, the 'Tring First Stop' stall on the High Street gave lorry drivers free cups of tea and coffee.

The lost Roman town of Verulamium comes to life as an archaeologist and assistants uncover a mosaic in 1932. The floor had once been part of a villa dating from around 200 AD and the mosaic may depict a Celtic deity, lord of animals and nature. Successive excavations were to uncover parts of the baths, basilica and the second-century theatre.

At rest; a sketch of Mackerye End Farm, Wheathampstead.

INDEX